DYLAN FOX

Go Idioms and Best Practices For Developers

Contents

Introduction: Why Go?

G o, also known as Golang, is a modern programming language that has rapidly gained traction since its inception in 2007 by a team at Google, led by Robert Griesemer, Rob Pike, and Ken Thompson. Designed to address the limitations of existing languages in the context of large-scale software development, Go offers a blend of simplicity, performance, and efficiency that makes it an ideal choice for building robust, scalable applications.

Go is often described as a "language born out of frustration," addressing common pain points experienced by developers who work with complex, multi-core systems, high-concurrency applications, and large codebases. It strikes a fine balance between the performance of low-level languages like C or C++ and the simplicity and ease of use found in high-level languages like Python. But what really sets Go apart is its ability to make concurrent programming both easy to use and understand, a challenge that most modern languages struggle with.

In this chapter, we'll explore the evolution of Go, its standout features, and how you can embark on your learning path to mastering the language.

The Evolution of Go

Go was born out of the need for a language that could handle the growing complexities of software development at scale. In the mid-2000s, Google faced unique challenges with its massive infrastructure, where existing languages like Java, C++, and Python were falling short in terms of compilation times, performance, and concurrency handling.

The development of Go aimed to solve these key issues:

- **Compilation Time:** C++ and Java were notorious for their long compilation times, particularly when working with large-scale projects. Go was designed to compile quickly, even for large codebases.
- **Concurrency:** Existing languages struggled with writing clean and efficient concurrent code, a necessity for modern, distributed systems. Go introduced Goroutines and channels to make concurrency more intuitive and easy to implement.
- **Code Simplicity:** Languages like C++ and Java often led to complex, verbose code. Go emphasized simplicity and readability, removing features that encouraged unnecessary complexity.

Go officially launched in 2009, and by 2012, it had matured enough to be used in production environments. Its simplicity, speed, and ability to handle high concurrency made it the go-to language for cloud-native applications, microservices, and systems programming.

Today, Go is widely adopted by industry giants such as Google, Docker, Uber, Netflix, and Dropbox. It has become a language of choice for developers looking to build efficient, scalable, and maintainable systems with minimal overhead.

Key Features That Make Go Stand Out

1. **Simplicity and Readability** Go was designed to be easy to learn and use. Its syntax is clean, with a focus on reducing boilerplate code. By removing unnecessary language features, such as inheritance, operator overloading, and generics (at least initially), Go encourages developers to write straightforward, readable code. This simplicity leads to better maintainability, making Go an excellent choice for long-term projects.

2. **Built-in Concurrency** Concurrency is a core feature of Go, and it's built directly into the language through Goroutines and channels. Goroutines are lightweight threads that make concurrent programming much simpler compared to traditional threading models in languages like Java or Python. Channels provide a powerful mechanism for communication between Goroutines, allowing developers to build highly concurrent applications with minimal effort.

3. **Fast Compilation and Execution** One of Go's key strengths is its lightning-fast compilation time. Unlike languages like Java and C++, Go compiles code into machine language almost instantaneously, making the development process faster and more efficient. The language also compiles to native machine code, ensuring high performance comparable to C or C++, which is crucial for system-level programming and large-scale applications.

4. **Memory Safety and Garbage Collection** Go automatically manages memory through a garbage collector, significantly reducing the risk of memory leaks and pointer-related bugs that plague languages like C and C++. However, Go's garbage collector is designed to be efficient and fast, minimizing its impact on application performance.

5. **Strong Standard Library** Go's standard library is extensive, covering a wide range of functionalities like file I/O, networking, and HTTP servers. This rich library allows developers to build powerful applications without needing to rely on third-party packages. The inclusion of robust tools for building web servers and handling concurrency makes Go particularly well-suited for cloud-native applications and web services.

6. **Cross-Platform Compilation** Go's ability to compile to different platforms from a single codebase makes it an ideal choice for multi-platform development. With Go, developers can write their application once and deploy it to various platforms such as Linux, macOS, and Windows without significant changes to the code.

7. **Efficient Dependency Management** With the introduction of Go Modules, Go has a clean and efficient system for managing dependencies. This allows developers to easily manage third-party libraries while avoiding issues like version conflicts. Go's dependency management is simple, fast, and integrates seamlessly into the language's tooling.

8. **Static Typing with the Flexibility of Dynamic Languages** Go is statically typed, which means it catches many errors at compile time, but it also provides enough flexibility to feel dynamic in nature. Its type system avoids the verbosity of other statically typed languages, enabling developers to write cleaner and less error-prone code.

Target Audience and Learning Path

Who Should Learn Go?

Go is an ideal language for a wide range of developers, including:

- **Backend Developers:** If you work on APIs, microservices, or high-performance backend systems, Go's concurrency model and speed make it perfect for building scalable web services.
- **System Programmers:** Go's performance is comparable to C and C++, but with modern features like garbage collection and simple syntax. This makes it a strong candidate for system-level programming.
- **DevOps Engineers:** Go is the language behind many DevOps tools (like Docker and Kubernetes), and its cross-platform nature and ease of use make it an essential language for automating infrastructure and managing cloud environments.
- **Cloud-Native Developers:** Go's standard library, concurrency model, and cross-compilation features make it a top choice for building cloud-

native applications and distributed systems.

- **Beginner Developers:** With its simple syntax and straightforward design, Go is a great language for beginners who want to dive into software engineering and build solid, maintainable codebases from the start.

Learning Path

1. **Familiarize Yourself with Go's Syntax and Tooling** Start by installing Go and setting up your development environment. Write simple programs to get comfortable with Go's syntax, including basic control structures, functions, and error handling.

2. **Master Go's Unique Features** Dive deeper into Goroutines, channels, and Go's concurrency model. Learn how to manage dependencies using Go Modules and explore the standard library for handling file I/O, networking, and HTTP.

3. **Build Real-World Projects** Practice by building real-world applications, such as APIs, CLI tools, or small web services. This will help you grasp Go's strengths in managing performance, concurrency, and large-scale system development.

4. **Understand Advanced Go Concepts** Explore Go's memory model, garbage collection, and optimization techniques. Learn how to profile and benchmark Go code to ensure you are writing efficient and scalable applications.

5. **Contribute to the Go Community** As you gain confidence, contribute to open-source projects or create your own libraries and tools. The Go community is active and supportive, providing plenty of opportunities to grow as a Go developer.

Chapter 1: Getting Started with Go

Setting Up Your Go Environment
Before writing your first Go program, you need to set up a proper development environment. Go's installation process is straightforward, and you'll be ready to code in no time. Here's a step-by-step guide to getting started.

1.1 Installing Go

Go is available for multiple platforms, including Windows, macOS, and Linux. You can download the latest stable release of Go from the official website golang.org.

Step-by-Step Installation Process:

1. **Download Go**
2. Visit the Go downloads page and select the appropriate version for your operating system. The installation file will be available for Windows (.msi), macOS (.pkg), or Linux (tar.gz).
3. **Installing on Windows**

- Download the .msi installer and run the file.
- Follow the prompts to complete the installation process.
- By default, Go will be installed in C:\Go, and the Go workspace will be set up in your user directory (%USERPROFILE%\go).

1. **Installing on macOS**

- Download the .pkg installer.
- Double-click the package and follow the installation instructions.
- Go is typically installed in /usr/local/go.

1. **Installing on Linux**

- Download the .tar.gz file.
- Extract the archive to /usr/local:

```bash
Copy code
tar -C /usr/local -xzf go1.x.x.linux-amd64.tar.gz
```

- Add Go's bin directory to your PATH by editing your shell profile (~/.bashrc or ~/.zshrc):

```bash
Copy code
export PATH=$PATH:/usr/local/go/bin
```

- Run source ~/.bashrc or restart your terminal to apply the changes.

1. **Verify Installation** After installation, verify that Go has been installed correctly. Open your terminal or command prompt and type:

```bash
Copy code
go version
```

1. You should see the Go version printed, confirming that the installation was successful.

1.2 Setting Up Your Workspace

Once Go is installed, you'll need to set up your Go workspace. The Go workspace is where your projects and source files will reside. By default, your workspace is located in your user directory under a folder called go.

Go Workspace Directory Structure:

- **bin/**: Contains executable binaries compiled by Go.
- **pkg/**: Contains compiled package objects.
- **src/**: Contains your source code.

You can create a workspace manually if it doesn't already exist:

```bash
Copy code
mkdir -p $HOME/go/{bin,pkg,src}
```

Go modules, introduced in version 1.11, simplify dependency management and allow you to create Go projects outside of your GOPATH. With modules, your workspace can be anywhere on your system, and each project will manage its dependencies using a go.mod file.

1.3 Setting Up Your Editor

To write and manage Go code efficiently, you'll want to set up a code editor with Go support. Here are some popular editors for Go development:

- **Visual Studio Code (VS Code)**: One of the most popular editors for Go development. You can install the official Go extension, which provides linting, syntax highlighting, debugging, and more.

- Install the Go extension by searching for "Go" in the Extensions Marketplace.
- After installation, the extension will prompt you to install additional tools for code analysis, testing, and debugging.
- **GoLand**: A dedicated IDE for Go, developed by JetBrains. It provides rich code navigation, debugging, and refactoring tools tailored for Go developers.
- **Vim or Neovim**: For those who prefer using terminal-based editors, Go support can be added to Vim using plugins like vim-go or coc-go.

Once you have set up your environment and workspace, you are ready to dive into Go's syntax and structure.

Understanding Go's Syntax and Structure

Go's syntax is designed for simplicity and readability. It's much less verbose compared to languages like Java or C++, which makes it easier to pick up, especially for developers new to programming.

2.1 Basic Syntax Overview

Here's a basic Go program to understand its structure:

```go
Copy code
package main

import "fmt"

func main() {
    fmt.Println("Hello, Go!")
}
```

Let's break this down:

- **Package Declaration**: The first line package main defines the package this file belongs to. In Go, every file belongs to a package, and the main

9

package is special because it's used for programs that can be executed. For libraries, you will use other package names.

- **Imports**: The import "fmt" statement imports a package by its path. In this case, the fmt package is used for formatted I/O (input/output) operations.
- **Functions**: The func main() defines the main function, which is the entry point of the Go program. All executable Go programs must have a main function.
- **Statements**: Inside the main function, fmt.Println("Hello, Go!") prints a string to the console. This is Go's way of handling formatted output.

2.2 Variable Declaration

Go has strong, static typing, but its variable declaration syntax is designed to be simple. Variables can be declared using the var keyword or the shorthand := syntax.

```go
Copy code
package main

import "fmt"

func main() {
    // Declaring variables with the var keyword
    var name string = "Alice"
    var age int = 30

    // Short variable declaration
    message := "Hello, Go!"
    fmt.Println(message, name, age)
}
```

- **var keyword**: Declares a variable with a specific type. Go requires all variables to have a type, either explicitly or inferred.
- **Shorthand :=:** Go allows shorthand declaration and initialization

without specifying the type; the type is inferred by the compiler.

2.3 Constants

Constants are declared using the const keyword and cannot be changed once assigned.

```go
Copy code
package main

import "fmt"

func main() {
    const pi = 3.14
    fmt.Println("The value of pi is:", pi)
}
```

2.4 Data Types

Go supports several basic data types:

- **Integers**: int, int8, int16, int32, int64
- **Unsigned Integers**: uint, uint8, uint16, uint32, uint64
- **Floating Point**: float32, float64
- **Strings**: string
- **Booleans**: bool

```go
Copy code
package main

import "fmt"

func main() {
    var x int = 5
    var y float64 = 42.5
```

```go
    var z bool = true
    var message string = "Go is great!"

    fmt.Println(x, y, z, message)
}
```

2.5 Control Structures

Go provides standard control structures like conditional statements and loops.

- **If-Else Statements**:

```go
go
Copy code
package main

import "fmt"

func main() {
    x := 10

    if x > 5 {
        fmt.Println("x is greater than 5")
    } else {
        fmt.Println("x is less than or equal to 5")
    }
}
```

- **For Loops**: The for loop is the only looping construct in Go, but it can be used in different ways.

```go
go
Copy code
package main

import "fmt"

func main() {
    for i := 0; i < 5; i++ {
        fmt.Println(i)
    }

    // Infinite loop
    for {
        fmt.Println("Looping...")
        break
    }
}
```

- **Switch Statements**:

```go
go
Copy code
package main

import "fmt"

func main() {
    day := 3

    switch day {
    case 1:
        fmt.Println("Monday")
    case 2:
        fmt.Println("Tuesday")
    case 3:
        fmt.Println("Wednesday")
```

```
    default:
        fmt.Println("Invalid day")
    }
}
```

2.6 Functions and Parameters

Functions in Go are first-class citizens, meaning they can be passed around as arguments, assigned to variables, and returned from other functions. A function in Go is defined using the func keyword.

```go
Copy code
package main

import "fmt"

// Function without parameters
func greet() {
    fmt.Println("Hello, Go!")
}

// Function with parameters
func add(a int, b int) int {
    return a + b
}

func main() {
    greet()
    sum := add(3, 4)
    fmt.Println("Sum:", sum)
}
```

Chapter 2: Idiomatic Go

G o is more than just a programming language—it's a set of best practices and philosophies aimed at building efficient, maintainable, and scalable software. One of the reasons for Go's rapid adoption across various industries is its focus on simplicity and clarity, often summed up by the phrase "less is more." In this chapter, we will explore the idiomatic use of Go and how adhering to its core principles results in cleaner, more reliable code.

Embracing Go's Philosophy: Less is More

At its core, Go promotes simplicity. While many modern languages offer a wide variety of features, Go was designed with the belief that fewer features often lead to clearer, more maintainable code. This philosophy manifests in several ways:

Minimalism in Language Features

Go avoids the complexity of multiple inheritance, operator overloading, and explicit error codes. Its designers intentionally left out features that might lead to complex abstractions and instead focused on making the language clear, concise, and to the point. This lack of "bells and whistles" is a feature, not a bug, and it's essential to embrace it to write idiomatic Go code.

For example:

- **No Generics** (until Go 1.18): Unlike languages like C++ or Java, Go historically didn't have generics. This design choice was made to avoid the complexity generics often introduce, though Go's recent updates have cautiously introduced them in a simplified manner.

- **No Implicit Conversions**: Go requires explicit conversions between types, which minimizes ambiguity in the code.

The Power of Composition Over Inheritance

Instead of supporting traditional inheritance, Go uses **composition** to promote flexible and reusable code. Structs can embed other structs, inheriting their fields and methods, which promotes a cleaner separation of concerns.

```go
Copy code
type Animal struct {
    Name string
}

type Dog struct {
    Animal // Embedding Animal struct
    Breed string
}

func main() {
    d := Dog{Animal: Animal{Name: "Buddy"}, Breed: "Golden
    Retriever"}
    fmt.Println(d.Name) // Inherits Name from Animal
}
```

Focus on Readability and Maintainability

Go values readability over cleverness. It's common to say that Go code should be written for others to read, rather than optimized for clever tricks. By focusing on simplicity, Go minimizes the cognitive load for developers, making it easier to maintain and extend codebases.

Key Aspects of Idiomatic Go:

- **Fewer Lines, More Meaning**: Write concise but meaningful code.

- **Be Explicit**: Avoid magic numbers, avoid global variables, and always be clear about what your code is doing.
- **Make Use of the Go Tooling**: Tools like go fmt and go vet are essential for enforcing Go's style and avoiding common pitfalls. Use them liberally.

Error Handling: The Go Way

Error handling in Go is significantly different from many other languages. Instead of exceptions, Go uses a simple, explicit mechanism based on return values. This might seem like a step back from exceptions or try-catch blocks, but it encourages developers to deal with errors right away, leading to more robust software.

Returning Errors Explicitly

In Go, functions that can fail return an error as their last return value. This requires developers to handle errors explicitly, rather than letting them propagate unnoticed.

```go
Copy code
func divide(a, b float64) (float64, error) {
    if b == 0 {
        return 0, fmt.Errorf("cannot divide by zero")
    }
    return a / b, nil
}

func main() {
    result, err := divide(4, 0)
    if err != nil {
        fmt.Println("Error:", err)
        return
    }
    fmt.Println("Result:", result)
}
```

- **Explicit over Implicit**: There's no automatic propagation of errors,

17

forcing you to handle each error where it occurs.

- **Error Wrapping**: Go 1.13 introduced error wrapping, which allows you to add context to errors while keeping the original error intact.

```go
Copy code
if err != nil {
    return fmt.Errorf("divide failed: %w", err)
}
```

This wrapping makes debugging easier, as it provides more context about where an error originated without losing the original error information.

Idiomatic Error Handling Patterns

1. Early Return on Errors One of the most common idioms in Go is to handle errors early and return immediately, rather than nesting if statements.

```go
Copy code
func process() error {
    result, err := doSomething()
    if err != nil {
        return err
    }

    // Continue with result
    return nil
}
```

This approach keeps the code flat and more readable.

2. Error Types and Custom Errors Sometimes you need to define more specific errors. Go allows you to create custom error types, which can be helpful when you want to handle certain errors in a special way.

```go
Copy code
type CustomError struct {
    Message string
    Code    int
}

func (e *CustomError) Error() string {
    return fmt.Sprintf("%d: %s", e.Code, e.Message)
}
```

Custom errors can include more context and even additional data like status codes or messages.

Error Logging

When you encounter an error, it's often helpful to log it. Go's standard library includes the log package, which allows you to log errors for debugging.

```go
Copy code
func main() {
    _, err := divide(4, 0)
    if err != nil {
        log.Println("Error occurred:", err)
    }
}
```

By making error handling explicit and consistent, Go ensures that errors don't get swept under the rug and encourages robust handling at every stage of program execution.

Goroutines and Channels: Idiomatic Concurrency

One of Go's standout features is its built-in concurrency model. Unlike traditional languages that use OS threads, Go provides **goroutines**, which are lightweight, managed threads that allow developers to write concurrent code easily.

Goroutines: Lightweight Threads

A goroutine is a function that runs concurrently with other goroutines. It's much lighter than an OS thread, allowing you to create thousands or even millions of goroutines without overwhelming system resources.

To create a goroutine, simply prefix a function call with the go keyword:

```go
Copy code
func sayHello() {
    fmt.Println("Hello!")
}

func main() {
    go sayHello() // This runs in a separate goroutine
    fmt.Println("Main function")
}
```

In the example above, the sayHello() function runs concurrently with the rest of the program. However, goroutines do not guarantee that they will finish before the main function exits, so synchronization is necessary for more complex use cases.

Channels: Communicating Between Goroutines

Channels provide a way for goroutines to communicate with each other. They are typed, meaning you can create a channel that only passes certain data types.

To create a channel:

```go
Copy code
ch := make(chan int)
```

You can send data to a channel using the <- operator:

```go
Copy code
```

```
ch <- 42
```

To receive data from a channel:

```go
Copy code
x := <-ch
```

Here's an example of goroutines and channels working together:

```go
Copy code
func add(a, b int, result chan int) {
    result <- a + b
}

func main() {
    result := make(chan int)

    go add(2, 3, result)
    sum := <-result

    fmt.Println("Sum:", sum)
}
```

In this example, the add function sends the sum of a and b through the channel, and the main function receives it.

Buffered and Unbuffered Channels

- **Unbuffered channels**: Require both the sender and receiver to be ready before the communication can proceed. If a goroutine sends a value on an unbuffered channel, it waits until another goroutine receives that value.
- **Buffered channels**: Allow you to specify a capacity. A goroutine can send up to the capacity of the channel without blocking.

```go
go
Copy code
ch := make(chan int, 2) // A buffered channel with capacity of 2
```

Select: Multiplexing Channels

The select statement allows a goroutine to wait on multiple communication operations. It is often used when you have multiple channels and need to handle whichever one is ready.

```go
go
Copy code
func main() {
    ch1 := make(chan string)
    ch2 := make(chan string)

    go func() { ch1 <- "hello from channel 1" }()
    go func() { ch2 <- "hello from channel 2" }()

    select {
    case msg1 := <-ch1:
        fmt.Println(msg1)
    case msg2 := <-ch2:
        fmt.Println(msg2)
    }
}
```

In this example, the select statement will wait for the first channel to be ready and print its value.

Synchronization with sync Package

Go also provides synchronization primitives like WaitGroup, Mutex, and Once in the sync package for cases where you need to coordinate more complex interactions between goroutines.

```go
Copy code
var wg sync.WaitGroup

func worker(id int) {
    defer wg.Done()
    fmt.Printf("Worker %d is starting\n", id)
}

func main() {
    wg.Add(1)
    go worker(1)
    wg.Wait() // Wait for the goroutines to finish
}
```

The sync.WaitGroup is used to wait for multiple goroutines to finish before allowing the program to exit.

Interfaces in Go: Decoupling and Flexibility

Go's type system is designed for simplicity, and one of its most powerful features is **interfaces**. Interfaces in Go are implicit, meaning that a type doesn't have to explicitly declare that it implements an interface. Instead, if a type provides the methods that an interface requires, it is automatically considered to implement that interface.

Defining and Implementing Interfaces

An interface is defined using the type keyword followed by a list of methods that any type implementing the interface must provide.

```go
Copy code
type Animal interface {
    Speak() string
}

type Dog struct{}

func (d Dog) Speak() string {
```

```
    return "Woof"
}

func main() {
    var a Animal = Dog{}
    fmt.Println(a.Speak()) // Outputs: Woof
}
```

In the example above, the Dog type implements the Animal interface by defining the Speak method. No explicit declaration is necessary.

Interface Usage in Go

Interfaces provide flexibility by allowing you to write functions that operate on different types, as long as they implement the required methods. This is particularly useful for writing modular, decoupled code.

```go
Copy code
type Cat struct{}

func (c Cat) Speak() string {
    return "Meow"
}

func speakToAnimal(a Animal) {
    fmt.Println(a.Speak())
}

func main() {
    speakToAnimal(Dog{})
    speakToAnimal(Cat{})
}
```

Here, speakToAnimal can take any type that implements the Animal interface, making it flexible and reusable.

Empty Interface: interface{}

The empty interface, interface{}, can represent any type. This allows you to write functions that accept any type as a parameter, similar to the use of

Object in languages like Java.

```go
Copy code
func describe(i interface{}) {
    fmt.Printf("Type: %T, Value: %v\n", i, i)
}


func main() {
    describe(42)
    describe("Hello")
}
```

While the empty interface is powerful, it's often recommended to use more specific interfaces to maintain type safety and clarity.

Type Assertions

When working with interfaces, you may need to convert the interface back to its concrete type. This is done using type assertions.

```go
Copy code
func main() {
    var i interface{} = "hello"

    s, ok := i.(string)
    if ok {
        fmt.Println(s)
    } else {
        fmt.Println("Not a string")
    }
}
```

In this example, we assert that the value of i is a string, and check whether the assertion is successful.

Decoupling with Interfaces

Interfaces in Go allow you to decouple your code, making it easier to swap out implementations without modifying your codebase. For example, if you're writing a logging system, you can define an interface for logging and provide different implementations for different loggers (file-based, cloud-based, etc.).

Chapter 3: Go Project Structure and Organization

Organizing your Go projects properly is essential for maintainability, scalability, and clarity. A well-organized project structure makes it easier for you and your collaborators to navigate the codebase and ensure long-term stability. In this chapter, we'll explore how to set up Go projects, best practices for structuring them, and how to organize your code for maintainability.

The GOPATH and Modules

Go has undergone an evolution in how it manages project organization and dependencies. In early versions, Go projects were governed by the GOPATH, which imposed certain constraints on how projects were structured. However, with the introduction of Go Modules in version 1.11, project organization became more flexible and easier to manage.

The GOPATH (Pre-Modules Era)

Before Go Modules, Go required a specific workspace structure that followed the GOPATH. The GOPATH environment variable defined the root directory where all Go projects and dependencies resided. This workspace had a predefined structure:

- **src/**: All source code files for your projects and dependencies.
- **bin/**: Compiled binaries for your Go programs.

- **pkg/**: Compiled package objects, especially for dependencies.

A typical GOPATH workspace looked like this:

```
css
Copy code
GOPATH/ ├───────
  bin/ ├──────
  pkg/ └──────
  src/ ├──────
      github.com/ │  └────────
        yourusername/ │  └───────
          yourproject/ ├──────
      golang.org/ └──────
      other-vendor/
```

While this structure helped organize code, it imposed limitations:

- You had to place your projects under the src directory.
- Managing dependencies manually was a challenge, often requiring tools like dep or glide.

Go Modules (The Modern Way)

Go Modules were introduced to overcome these limitations. Modules provide a way to manage dependencies and versioning in a more flexible and scalable way. They allow projects to reside anywhere on your filesystem, removing the requirement for the GOPATH workspace structure.

Modules are defined by a go.mod file that tracks dependencies and versions. Here's an example of what a go.mod file looks like:

```bash
Copy code
module github.com/yourusername/yourproject
```

```
go 1.18

require (
    github.com/some/dependency v1.2.3
    golang.org/x/tools v0.1.2
)
```

How to Initialize a Go Module: To initialize a module, simply run:

```bash
bash
Copy code
go mod init github.com/yourusername/yourproject
```

This creates a go.mod file, and from here, Go will automatically track your project's dependencies.

Key Benefits of Go Modules:

- **No More GOPATH Restrictions**: Your project can live anywhere on your machine.
- **Dependency Versioning**: Go Modules provide fine-grained version control over your dependencies.
- **Simpler Dependency Management**: Modules automatically manage downloading, upgrading, and ensuring dependencies are compatible with your project.

Go Modules simplify and modernize the process of managing dependencies, making it the recommended approach for all Go projects moving forward.

Best Practices for Project Layout

A well-structured project layout is key to ensuring your Go codebase is maintainable and scalable. There's no strict "one size fits all" approach to organizing Go projects, but over time, the Go community has developed some best practices that you can adopt for different types of applications.

Standard Project Layout

One commonly adopted project structure follows a standard approach that separates key concerns into directories. Here's an example:

```
go
Copy code
yourproject/
  cmd/
      yourapp/
          main.go
  internal/
      app/
          handler.go
          service.go
  pkg/
      util/
          helpers.go
  api/
      models/
      routes.go
  config/
      config.go
  go.mod
  go.sum
```

Let's break down this structure:

- **cmd/**: This directory contains the entry point for your application. If you have multiple applications (e.g., CLI tools, services), each can reside in its own subdirectory under cmd/. For example, the main package for your app would be cmd/yourapp/main.go.
- **internal/**: The internal directory is reserved for private packages that should not be imported by external projects. This directory is useful for organizing application-specific logic, such as services, handlers, and core business rules.
- **pkg/**: The pkg directory is used for shared libraries and utilities that could potentially be used by external applications. Think of this as the

home for reusable code that doesn't contain application-specific logic.

- **api/**: This directory contains definitions for API routes and models. You can define your data models, route handlers, and other API-related logic here.
- **config/**: Configuration files and settings, such as environment variables or initialization logic, live in this directory. It ensures that configuration is separate from the core application logic.

Organizing Code by Domain

Another effective strategy is organizing code based on the application's domain. For example, if you're building an e-commerce platform, you might have domain-specific directories:

```go
Copy code
yourproject/ ├───────
  cmd/ ├───────
  internal/ │ ├───────
    user/ │ │ └───────
        user.go │ ├───────
    product/ │ │ └───────
        product.go │ ├───────
    order/ │ │ └───────
        order.go └───────
  go.mod
```

In this structure:

- Each domain (user, product, order) gets its own directory inside internal/. This separation ensures that the logic for each domain is independent, making it easier to maintain and scale your codebase.
- Domain-specific packages handle their respective concerns (e.g., the user domain handles user authentication, profiles, etc.).

Monorepos and Multi-Service Architectures

For large organizations or projects with multiple services and microservices, it's common to adopt a monorepo structure where all services are kept within the same repository. Go Modules allow each service to have its own go.mod file, making it possible to manage dependencies separately for each service.

Here's a simplified structure for a monorepo with multiple microservices:

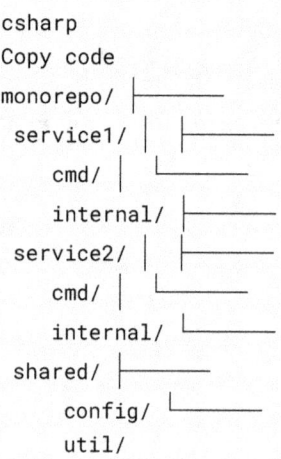

```
csharp
Copy code
monorepo/
  service1/
    cmd/
    internal/
  service2/
    cmd/
    internal/
  shared/
    config/
    util/
```

Each service has its own directory and module, while shared libraries or utilities are kept in the shared/ directory.

Organizing Your Code for Maintainability

As your Go project grows, maintaining clean code becomes critical for preventing technical debt. A few key practices can help you keep your codebase organized and maintainable:

1. Separation of Concerns

One of the guiding principles in software development is the **separation of concerns**. This means that different parts of your application should have distinct responsibilities. In Go, this can be achieved by separating business logic from presentation logic and infrastructure code.

For example, if you're building a web service, you might separate routing, business logic, and data access into different packages or layers:

- **Routing Layer**: Handles incoming HTTP requests and passes them to the appropriate services.
- **Service Layer**: Contains the core business logic.
- **Data Access Layer**: Interacts with databases, file systems, or external APIs.

This modular approach ensures that changes in one area (such as switching from one database to another) don't impact the entire codebase.

2. Consistent Package Naming

Go encourages organizing code into packages. A key part of organizing your project for maintainability is choosing consistent and descriptive package names. Good package names should describe what the package does, not how it does it.

For example, instead of naming a package utils, which is too generic and vague, you might name it strings if it provides string manipulation functions.

Guidelines for Package Naming:

- **Avoid overly generic names**: Instead of helpers or utils, use descriptive names like validation or httpclient.
- **Keep package names short and lowercase**: In Go, package names should be short and in lowercase without underscores.
- **Avoid repetition**: Don't repeat the package name in your functions or types. For example, if you have a package user, avoid naming a struct User inside it; just name it Struct.

3. Decoupling with Interfaces

Go's interfaces are key to writing maintainable and testable code. By defining interfaces for components of your system, you can decouple implementations from the higher-level logic that depends on them.

For instance, if you have a service that needs to send emails, you can define an EmailSender interface and pass the implementation in at runtime:

```go
go
Copy code
type EmailSender interface {
    Send(to string, subject string,
 body string) error
}

type emailService struct{}

func (e *emailService) Send
(to, subject, body string) error {
    // Logic to send email
    return nil
}

func notifyUser(s EmailSender, user string) {
    s.Send(user, "Welcome",
"Thanks for signing up!")
}
```

This approach makes it easy to swap out the email sending implementation (for example, when switching from a mock to a production service) without changing the rest of the codebase.

4. Testing and Code Coverage

Testing is an essential part of writing maintainable code. Go's testing framework is built into the language, making it easy to write unit tests for each package.

Organize your tests: Place tests in the same package as the code they are testing. For example, if you have a file user.go, the tests should live in user_test.go within the same directory.

Table-Driven Tests: Go idiomatic tests often use **table-driven testing**, which allows you to test multiple cases in a single test function. This helps reduce duplication and makes tests easier to maintain.

```go
go
Copy code
func TestAdd(t *testing.T) {
    cases := []struct{
        a, b int
        expected int
    }{
        {1, 2, 3},
        {5, 6, 11},
        {0, 0, 0},
    }

    for _, c := range cases {
        result := Add(c.a, c.b)
        if result != c.expected {
            t.Errorf("Add(%d, %d)
== %d, expected %d",
c.a, c.b, result, c.expected)
        }
    }
}
```

By writing comprehensive tests and ensuring code coverage, you make it easier to refactor your code without introducing bugs.

Conclusion

By adopting Go Modules and following best practices for project structure, you can create scalable and maintainable Go projects. A clean, well-organized codebase ensures that as your project grows, it remains easy to navigate, test, and extend. Embrace Go's philosophy of simplicity, organize your packages thoughtfully, and ensure a clear separation of concerns to build projects that stand the test of time.

Chapter 4: Writing Readable and Efficient Go Code

Writing readable and efficient code is fundamental to building maintainable and scalable applications. In Go, readability and efficiency are deeply ingrained into the language's design. Go emphasizes simplicity, code clarity, and correctness. This chapter will dive into Go's best practices for naming conventions, code clarity, effective use of comments, and leveraging Go's built-in tools (gofmt, go vet) to write code that's both performant and easy to maintain.

Naming Conventions and Code Clarity

In Go, naming conventions are critical for code readability. Well-chosen names make code easier to understand, maintain, and work on collaboratively. Following idiomatic Go naming conventions will help ensure consistency and clarity throughout your codebase.

1. Simplicity and Descriptive Names

Go encourages simple, descriptive names. Variables, functions, and types should have names that clearly convey their purpose. While concise names are preferred, they should never sacrifice clarity.

Examples of clear naming:

- Use message instead of msg or m
- Use startTime instead of st

- Use userProfile instead of up

Go idioms for naming:

- **For local variables**: Short and concise names, especially in short scopes, are encouraged.

```go
Copy code
for i := 0; i < n; i++ { //
'i' is clear within a short loop
    // ...
}
```

- **For global variables**: Names should be more descriptive, as they may be used across packages.

```go
Copy code
var maxConnections = 100 // more descriptive for global usage
```

2. CamelCase and Naming Style

Go uses **CamelCase** (also called mixed case) for naming. For example:

- **Exported Names**: Begin with an uppercase letter, making them accessible outside the package.

```go
Copy code
```

```
func FetchData() {} // Can be used in other packages
```

- **Unexported Names**: Begin with a lowercase letter, making them private to the package.

```go
Copy code
func fetchData() {} // Only used within the same package
```

3. Avoid Overly Long Names

While names should be descriptive, they should not be unnecessarily verbose. Strike a balance between clarity and brevity. For example:

- **Bad**: calculateTotalCostIncludingTaxAndDiscount
- **Good**: calculateTotal

4. Avoid Redundancy in Names

There's no need to repeat the type in the name, as Go's strong typing already provides clarity. For example:

- **Bad**: userStruct or userUser
- **Good**: user

5. Function Names Should Reflect Actions

Function names should clearly describe what they do, typically using verbs for actions:

- **Bad**: data()
- **Good**: fetchData(), updateUser(), sendEmail()

6. Constants and Package-Level Variables

- Constants should be named using uppercase letters and underscores (ALL_CAPS), but Go tends to prefer CamelCase for exported constants, as it's consistent with function and type naming.

```go
Copy code
const MaxRetries = 5
```

Effective Use of Go Comments

Comments play an important role in making your code more understandable, especially for others who may work on it later. However, Go encourages you to write **self-documenting code**—code that's clear enough that it needs minimal commenting. When comments are necessary, they should be concise, accurate, and placed effectively.

1. Documentation Comments

In Go, documentation comments are used to describe packages, types, functions, and methods. These comments are placed directly above the declaration and follow a specific style.

- **Package comments** should provide an overview of the package's functionality and are written directly above the package keyword.

```go
Copy code
// Package math provides basic constants and mathematical
functions.
package math
```

- **Function and method comments** should explain what the function does and describe its parameters and return values (if necessary). These comments are essential for any exported function or method.

```go
Copy code
// Add returns the sum of two integers.
func Add(a, b int) int {
    return a + b
}
```

2. Inline Comments

Inline comments can be used to clarify complex or non-obvious code, but they should not restate what the code already makes clear.

- **Good inline comment**:

```go
Copy code
x := 10
y := x + 5 // increment by 5 to account for offset
```

- **Avoid redundant comments**:

```go
Copy code
x := 10 // declare variable x and set it to 10 (redundant)
```

3. TODO Comments

You can use TODO comments to indicate future work or areas of the code that need improvement. In Go, the standard practice is to prefix TODO comments with TODO:.

```go
go
Copy code
// TODO: Refactor this function to handle edge cases
func processData() {
    // code...
}
```

4. Avoid Over-Commenting

Go encourages minimal commenting, only where necessary. Don't explain code that's already self-explanatory. If you find yourself writing a lot of comments, it might be an indication that your code could be made clearer.

Code Formatting with gofmt and go vet

Go comes with powerful built-in tools to ensure that code is properly formatted and free of basic issues. Consistency in formatting is vital for readability, especially when multiple developers are working on the same codebase.

1. gofmt: Automatic Code Formatting

One of Go's best features is gofmt, a tool that automatically formats your code to match the style expected by the Go community. By using gofmt, you ensure that all code adheres to Go's standard formatting guidelines, avoiding unnecessary debates about code style.

Usage:

```bash
bash
Copy code
gofmt -w myfile.go
```

- The -w flag writes the changes directly to the file.
- gofmt removes extraneous spaces, aligns indentation, and ensures consistent use of tabs.

Benefits of using gofmt:

- **Consistency**: All Go code looks the same, regardless of the developer.
- **Readability**: Properly formatted code is easier to read and understand.
- **Collaboration**: It eliminates disputes over formatting in code reviews.

2. go vet: Catching Common Mistakes

go vet is a static analysis tool that checks for common coding mistakes that the compiler won't catch. It helps identify potential bugs, misuse of API functions, or performance issues that could arise.

Common checks performed by go vet:

- **Printf-style functions**: Ensures that the number of arguments and format specifiers match in functions like fmt.Printf.
- **Unused variables**: Warns about variables that are declared but never used.
- **Struct tags**: Checks the syntax of struct field tags for validity.

Usage:

```bash
Copy code
go vet ./...
```

- This command runs go vet on all packages in the current directory.

Example:

```go
Copy code
func Example() {
    fmt.Printf("%d", "string") // mismatched type
}
```

go vet will flag this as an error, as "string" doesn't match the %d format

42

specifier.

Avoiding Common Go Code Smells

Code smells are indicators that there may be underlying problems in your code, making it harder to maintain or extend. By avoiding these common Go code smells, you can ensure your code remains clean and maintainable.

1. Overuse of Global Variables

Global variables are accessible from anywhere in your code, making them difficult to track and modify. Overusing global variables can lead to unintended side effects and obscure bugs. Instead, prefer passing variables through function parameters or using dependency injection.

Bad:

```go
Copy code
var globalCounter int

func increment() {
    globalCounter++
}
```

Good:

```go
Copy code
func increment(counter *int) {
    *counter++
}
```

2. Duplicated Code

Code duplication is a common smell that increases maintenance effort. If you find yourself duplicating code, refactor it into a function or package that can be reused.

Bad:

```go
Copy code
func addNumbers() int {
    return 1 + 2
}

func addOtherNumbers() int {
    return 3 + 4
}
```

Good:

```go
Copy code
func add(a, b int) int {
    return a + b
}
```

3. Misuse of Goroutines

Goroutines are a powerful concurrency feature in Go, but they can easily lead to issues like race conditions, memory leaks, or excessive resource consumption if not managed correctly.

- **Avoid starting goroutines without a way to control them**: Always ensure you have proper synchronization or a mechanism to signal when goroutines should exit.

Bad:

```go
Copy code
go process() // No control over the lifecycle of the goroutine
```

Good:

```go
Copy code
done := make(chan bool)
go func() {
    process()
    done <- true
}()
<-done // Wait for the goroutine to finish
```

4. Ignoring Errors

One of the most common code smells in Go is ignoring errors. Go's explicit error handling is one of the language's strengths, and skipping error checks can lead to unnoticed bugs and crashes.

Bad:

```go
Copy code
result, _ := someFunction() // Ignoring the error
```

Good:

```go
Copy code
result, err := someFunction()
if err != nil {
    // handle error
}
```

5. Not Closing Resources

Go's defer keyword is often used to ensure resources like files, network connections, and database connections are closed after they are no longer needed. Forgetting to close resources can lead to memory leaks and resource exhaustion.

Bad:

```go
Copy code
f, err := os.Open("file.txt")
if err != nil {
    return
}
// forgetting to close the file
```

Good:

```go
Copy code
f, err := os.Open("file.txt")
if err != nil {
    return
}
defer f.Close()
```

By using defer, the f.Close() statement is guaranteed to execute when the surrounding function returns, ensuring that the file is properly closed.

Conclusion

Writing readable and efficient Go code is essential for building maintainable and scalable software. By following Go's idiomatic naming conventions, writing clear comments where necessary, and adhering to the formatting standards enforced by gofmt and go vet, you can produce clean, maintainable code. Additionally, by avoiding common code smells and staying mindful of best practices, you ensure that your Go projects remain robust and easy to maintain in the long run.

Chapter 5: Managing Dependencies in Go

Managing dependencies is a crucial part of any software project, and Go has evolved to make this process both straightforward and efficient. With the introduction of Go Modules, developers can now handle project dependencies more easily, with built-in support for versioning and external libraries. In this chapter, we will explore how Go Modules simplify dependency management, the best practices for using version control systems (VCS) with Go, and how to work effectively with external libraries and packages.

Go Modules: Dependency Management Simplified

Go Modules represent a significant shift from the early days of Go, where dependency management was tied to the GOPATH and manually tracked. Modules provide a more modern, flexible, and streamlined approach, enabling developers to manage project dependencies more easily, handle multiple versions of packages, and maintain a clear project structure.

1. What are Go Modules?

Go Modules are a dependency management system that was introduced in Go 1.11 and became the default in Go 1.16. With Go Modules, each project can define its dependencies explicitly using a go.mod file, which lists all the modules (dependencies) and their specific versions that your project needs to function correctly. This means you are no longer bound by the GOPATH and can place your project anywhere on your system.

Key Benefits of Go Modules:
- **Decoupling from GOPATH**: You are free to store Go projects outside of the GOPATH directory.
- **Versioning**: Go Modules manage package versions, ensuring that your project uses compatible versions of dependencies.
- **Isolation**: Each project has its own set of dependencies, preventing conflicts across different projects.
- **Reproducibility**: Go Modules ensure consistent builds by locking dependencies to specific versions, improving reproducibility.

2. Setting Up Go Modules

To initialize a Go Module for your project, you need to run the go mod init command in the root of your project directory. This will create a go.mod file, which serves as the blueprint for managing dependencies.

Step-by-Step Guide:

1. **Create a new Go project**:

```bash
Copy code
mkdir myproject
cd myproject
```

1. **Initialize the module**:

```bash
Copy code
go mod init github.com/yourusername/myproject
```

1. This creates a go.mod file that looks like this:

48

```bash
bash
Copy code
module github.com/yourusername/myproject

go 1.18
```

1. **Adding dependencies**: Whenever you import a new package that isn't part of the standard library, Go Modules automatically add it to the go.mod file the first time you run go build, go run, or go test. For example:

```go
go
Copy code
import "github.com/gin-gonic/gin"
```

1. When you run go build, Go Modules will update the go.mod file with the required package and version:

```bash
bash
Copy code
require github.com/gin-gonic/gin v1.7.4
```

3. Managing Dependencies with Go Modules

Go Modules also manage a second file, go.sum, which tracks the exact versions of dependencies and their checksums for verification.

- **go.mod**: Defines the high-level dependencies and versions.
- **go.sum**: Ensures reproducibility by recording the cryptographic hashes

of the module's dependencies, preventing unauthorized or corrupted changes to the modules.

Command Overview:

- go mod tidy: Cleans up the go.mod file by removing any dependencies that are no longer required and adding any missing dependencies.
- go get <module>: Adds a new dependency or updates an existing one to the latest version.
- go mod download: Downloads all the modules specified in the go.mod file.
- go mod vendor: Copies dependencies into a vendor/ directory, allowing you to check them into version control if needed.

By using Go Modules, you avoid the challenges of manually managing dependencies and ensure your project is easy to build, share, and reproduce in any environment.

Using Versioning and VCS with Go

Version control is an essential practice in modern software development. Go's module system integrates seamlessly with version control systems (VCS) like Git, allowing you to manage package versions and collaborate on projects efficiently.

1. Versioning in Go Modules

Go Modules support semantic versioning (SemVer), which makes it easier to manage updates and changes in your dependencies. Semantic versioning uses a three-part number: **MAJOR.MINOR.PATCH**, where:

- **MAJOR**: Increases when there are incompatible API changes.
- **MINOR**: Increases when functionality is added in a backward-compatible manner.
- **PATCH**: Increases for backward-compatible bug fixes.

When adding or updating dependencies, Go Modules automatically select the latest patch version for a given minor version. However, you can explicitly specify a particular version if needed.

Specifying Versions:

- To install a specific version of a module, use:

```bash
Copy code
go get github.com/gin-gonic/gin@v1.7.0
```

- This pins your project to that specific version of the Gin web framework.

2. Go Modules and VCS Integration

When you create a Go project and use a VCS like Git, the go.mod file will automatically track all the dependencies, ensuring that any team member or system working on the project has the correct versions.

Best Practices for Version Control in Go Projects:

- **Commit the go.mod and go.sum files**: These files are essential for reproducibility and should always be committed to your version control system. They allow other developers to build your project with the exact same dependencies.
- **Don't commit the vendor folder unless necessary**: The vendor/ folder can be generated using go mod vendor if you need to include all dependencies in your repository, but in most cases, relying on go.mod and go.sum is sufficient.

3. Working with Private Repositories

Sometimes, you might want to use Go Modules to pull in packages from private repositories (e.g., private GitHub repositories or internal company repositories). Go supports fetching modules from private repositories using

Git authentication.

Accessing Private Repositories:

1. **Set up authentication**: Ensure your Git client is configured with the appropriate credentials (SSH or HTTPS with personal access tokens).
2. **Use Go Private**: Go's environment variable GOPRIVATE tells Go to avoid using the public module proxy and instead use your VCS directly. Set the GOPRIVATE variable to your private domain:

```bash
Copy code
export GOPRIVATE=github.
com/yourorganization/*
```

1. **Fetch private modules**: After setting GOPRIVATE, Go will fetch your private modules as it would any public dependency, ensuring that sensitive code is not shared with public proxies.

Working with External Libraries and Packages

Go thrives on a rich ecosystem of external libraries and packages that developers can use to extend the capabilities of their applications. Managing these external packages effectively is key to ensuring a stable and maintainable project.

1. Finding External Libraries

The Go community has developed a wide range of third-party libraries for different use cases, from web frameworks to database clients. Some popular places to find Go libraries include:

- **GoPkg**: A searchable database of Go packages.
- **GitHub**: Many open-source Go libraries are hosted on GitHub.
- **Go.dev**: The official package discovery site for Go libraries.

2. Adding External Libraries

To use an external library in your project, simply import it in your code and then run one of Go's build or test commands (go build, go run, or go test), which will automatically download and install the package as a module dependency.

Example: Using the gin-gonic/gin library:

1. **Import the package in your code**:

```go
Copy code
import "github.com/gin-gonic/gin"
```

1. **Run a Go command to download the package**:

```bash
Copy code
go build
```

1. This will update the go.mod file to include the Gin dependency.

3. Updating External Libraries

When working with external libraries, it's important to keep them up to date, especially when bug fixes and security patches are released. You can update dependencies using the go get command:

To update a specific dependency:

```
bash
Copy code
go get -u github.com/gin-gonic/gin
```

To update all dependencies:

```
bash
Copy code
go get -u ./...
```

4. Vendor Directory

In some cases, especially in enterprise environments, you may want to include all dependencies directly in your repository (e.g., for compliance or to ensure builds work without internet access). Go supports this via the vendor/ directory, which contains a copy of all external dependencies.

To vendor your dependencies:

```
bash
Copy code
go mod vendor
```

The vendor folder will now contain all of the external packages your project depends on. You can commit this directory to your repository if needed, though it's not commonly done for open-source projects.

5. Managing Transitive Dependencies

Transitive dependencies are dependencies of dependencies—libraries that your direct dependencies rely on. Go Modules automatically handle these for you, resolving the appropriate versions of transitive dependencies when you import a library.

If you run into issues with conflicting versions of transitive dependencies, Go provides commands to help resolve the conflicts:

- **go mod graph**: Visualizes the module dependency graph, showing how transitive dependencies relate to each other.

- **go mod tidy**: Cleans up unused dependencies and ensures that your go.mod file accurately reflects the dependencies your project needs.

Conclusion

Managing dependencies in Go has become much more streamlined and manageable with the introduction of Go Modules. By understanding how to initialize modules, handle versioning, and work with external libraries, you can build stable, reproducible Go projects. Additionally, using VCS integration ensures that your team can collaborate efficiently while maintaining consistent dependency versions. As your project evolves, staying on top of module updates and understanding the nuances of dependency management will ensure your Go applications remain robust and maintainable over time.

Chapter 6: Idiomatic Go Concurrency

Concurrency is one of Go's standout features, offering developers a simple yet powerful model for writing efficient, scalable programs. By leveraging goroutines, channels, and Go's synchronization primitives, you can efficiently manage multiple tasks simultaneously while keeping your code clean and maintainable. This chapter explores idiomatic Go concurrency, including goroutines, channel patterns, synchronization techniques, and strategies for avoiding common concurrency pitfalls.

Leveraging Goroutines for Efficient Concurrency

Goroutines are one of the core components of Go's concurrency model. They are lightweight threads managed by the Go runtime, allowing you to run multiple functions concurrently without the overhead of creating operating system (OS) threads. Goroutines are much cheaper than OS threads, making them ideal for handling tasks that involve waiting (e.g., I/O operations) and parallel execution.

1. What is a Goroutine?

A goroutine is simply a function that runs concurrently with other goroutines. You can start a goroutine by using the go keyword before a function call. Goroutines are non-blocking, meaning they can continue executing without waiting for other goroutines to finish.

```go
Copy code
package main

import (
    "fmt"
    "time"
)

func sayHello() {
    fmt.Println("Hello, Go!")
}

func main() {
    go sayHello()  // This runs as a goroutine
    time.Sleep(1 * time.Second) // Prevent the main function from
    exiting immediately
}
```

In the example above, sayHello runs concurrently with the rest of the program. However, the main function exits before sayHello completes, which is why we use time.Sleep to allow the goroutine to finish.

2. Goroutines vs Threads

Unlike traditional OS threads, which are heavyweight and limited in number, goroutines are extremely lightweight. The Go runtime can manage thousands (even millions) of goroutines within a single process. Goroutines are multiplexed onto a smaller number of OS threads, which allows Go to efficiently handle a large number of concurrent tasks.

3. When to Use Goroutines

- **I/O-bound tasks**: Use goroutines for tasks that involve waiting, such as reading from a network or file system.
- **Parallel tasks**: When you need to run multiple tasks at the same time (e.g., fetching data from multiple sources concurrently).
- **Background tasks**: Goroutines are perfect for running tasks in the

background while the main program continues executing.

Best practices:

- **Avoid running too many goroutines**: Even though goroutines are lightweight, creating millions of goroutines can overwhelm the Go runtime. Use them judiciously.
- **Manage goroutines' lifecycle**: Always ensure goroutines terminate when no longer needed. Leaving goroutines running can lead to resource leaks.

Channel Patterns and Best Practices

Channels are Go's way of synchronizing communication between goroutines. They provide a mechanism for goroutines to send and receive data, ensuring that concurrency is both safe and efficient.

1. What are Channels?

Channels are typed conduits through which you can send and receive values between goroutines. You create a channel using make, and you can send values to a channel using the <- operator.

```go
Copy code
package main

import "fmt"

func main() {
    ch := make(chan string)

    go func() {
        ch <- "Hello from goroutine!"
    }()

    message := <-ch
    fmt.Println(message)
```

```
}
```

In this example:

- A string channel (ch) is created.
- A goroutine sends a message into the channel.
- The main function waits to receive the message and prints it.

2. Buffered vs Unbuffered Channels

- **Unbuffered channels**: Both the sender and receiver must be ready at the same time for communication to occur. If a goroutine tries to send data on an unbuffered channel but no goroutine is ready to receive it, the sending goroutine will block.

```go
Copy code
ch := make(chan string) // Unbuffered
```

- **Buffered channels**: Allow you to specify a buffer size, meaning a goroutine can send values without immediately waiting for the receiver, up to the buffer capacity.

```go
Copy code
ch := make(chan string, 3) // Buffered with capacity of 3
```

Best practice: Use unbuffered channels when synchronization is needed and buffered channels when you want to decouple sender and receiver operations.

3. Common Channel Patterns

1. Fan-out/Fan-in Pattern

The fan-out/fan-in pattern is a way to distribute work across multiple goroutines (fan-out) and then aggregate the results (fan-in).

Fan-out Example:

```go
Copy code
func worker(id int, ch chan int) {
    ch <- id * 2
}

func main() {
    ch := make(chan int, 3)

    for i := 1; i <= 3; i++ {
        go worker(i, ch)
    }

    for i := 1; i <= 3; i++ {
        result := <-ch
        fmt.Println("Received:", result)
    }
}
```

In this example, multiple goroutines (workers) send results to the channel, and the main goroutine receives and processes them.

2. Select Statement

The select statement allows a goroutine to wait on multiple channels. It is useful when you want to handle multiple communication operations concurrently.

```go
Copy code
select {
case msg1 := <-ch1:
    fmt.Println("Received from ch1:", msg1)
case msg2 := <-ch2:
```

```
    fmt.Println("Received from ch2:", msg2)
}
```

Best practice: Always include a default case in the select statement when you want to avoid blocking forever.

4. Closing Channels

Channels should be closed when no more data will be sent. Closing a channel is essential for signaling to receivers that no further data will be sent.

```go
Copy code
close(ch)
```

Important note: Only the sender should close a channel. Closing from the receiver or closing an already closed channel causes a panic.

Synchronization Techniques with sync and atomic

While channels are the preferred way to manage concurrency in Go, there are situations where more explicit synchronization primitives are necessary. The sync and atomic packages provide tools for handling low-level synchronization tasks.

1. The sync.WaitGroup

The sync.WaitGroup is used to wait for a collection of goroutines to finish. It allows you to synchronize the completion of multiple goroutines before the main program continues.

Example using WaitGroup:

```go
Copy code
package main

import (
    "fmt"
    "sync"
```

```go
)

func worker(id int, wg *sync.WaitGroup) {
    defer wg.Done() //
 Mark the goroutine as done when it finishes
    fmt.Printf("Worker %d starting\n", id)
    // Do some work
    fmt.Printf("Worker %d done\n", id)
}

func main() {
    var wg sync.WaitGroup

    for i := 1; i <= 3; i++ {
        wg.Add(1) // Increment the WaitGroup counter
        go worker(i, &wg)
    }

    wg.Wait() // Block until all goroutines finish
}
```

2. The sync.Mutex

A **mutex** (mutual exclusion) is used to protect shared resources from concurrent access by multiple goroutines. Only one goroutine can hold a mutex at a time, ensuring safe access to the critical section.

Example using Mutex:

```go
go
Copy code
package main

import (
    "fmt"
    "sync"
)

type Counter struct {
    mu      sync.Mutex
```

```go
    count int
}

func (c *Counter) Increment() {
    c.mu.Lock()    // Lock the mutex before modifying shared state
    defer c.mu.Unlock() // Unlock after modification
    c.count++
}

func (c *Counter) Value() int {
    c.mu.Lock()
    defer c.mu.Unlock()
    return c.count
}

func main() {
    var wg sync.WaitGroup
    counter := Counter{}

    for i := 0; i < 1000; i++ {
        wg.Add(1)
        go func() {
            defer wg.Done()
            counter.Increment()
        }()
    }

    wg.Wait()
    fmt.Println("Final count:", counter.Value())
}
```

In this example, sync.Mutex ensures that only one goroutine modifies the count at any given time.

3. The sync.Once

sync.Once guarantees that a piece of code is executed only once, even if multiple goroutines attempt to run it simultaneously.

Example:

```go
go
Copy code
package main

import (
    "fmt"
    "sync"
)

var once sync.Once

func initialize() {
    fmt.Println("Initialization code running")
}

func main() {
    var wg sync.WaitGroup
    for i := 0; i < 3; i++ {
        wg.Add(1)
        go func() {
            defer wg.Done()
            once.Do(initialize)
// Initialization runs only once
        }()
    }
    wg.Wait()
}
```

4. The sync.Cond

sync.Cond is a more advanced synchronization primitive that provides broadcast-style communication among goroutines. It's useful when one or more goroutines must wait for a condition to be met before proceeding.

Avoiding Common Concurrency Pitfalls

Concurrency can be tricky, and there are a few common pitfalls you need to watch out for when writing concurrent Go code.

1. Race Conditions

A race condition occurs when multiple goroutines access shared resources simultaneously, leading to unpredictable behavior. Go provides a tool called race detector to help you identify race conditions.

To run the race detector:

```bash
Copy code
go run -race yourprogram.go
```

2. Goroutine Leaks

Goroutine leaks occur when a goroutine is created but never properly terminates, leading to resource exhaustion. To avoid this, make sure to handle the lifecycle of your goroutines properly, including implementing exit signals using channels.

3. Deadlocks

A deadlock happens when two or more goroutines are waiting indefinitely for each other to release resources. To prevent deadlocks, always ensure that resources are acquired and released in a consistent order, and use proper synchronization tools like sync.Mutex or channels.

Example of deadlock:

```go
Copy code
var mu1, mu2 sync.Mutex

go func() {
    mu1.Lock()
    mu2.Lock() // Deadlock if another goroutine holds mu2
}()
```

4. Oversynchronization

Avoid overuse of synchronization primitives like mutexes. In many cases, channels can provide a cleaner, less error-prone way to manage concurrency. Oversynchronization can also reduce performance by introducing unnecessary blocking.

Conclusion

Concurrency is a powerful feature in Go, and by using goroutines, channels, and synchronization primitives like sync and atomic, you can build highly efficient and scalable applications. By understanding key concurrency patterns and avoiding common pitfalls like race conditions and deadlocks, you'll be able to leverage Go's full potential for concurrent programming while maintaining clean, idiomatic code.

Chapter 7: Go Memory Management and Optimization

G o's memory management is one of its core strengths, balancing simplicity with performance. The language provides built-in garbage collection (GC) to handle memory automatically, but understanding how memory works in Go will help you optimize your programs and avoid issues like memory leaks. In this chapter, we will explore Go's memory model, how to work with pointers and values, techniques for profiling and benchmarking your code, and best practices for optimizing garbage collection.

Understanding Go's Memory Model

Go's memory model defines how memory is allocated, accessed, and managed during the execution of a program. It includes concepts like heap and stack allocation, garbage collection, and how Go manages memory safety. By understanding these concepts, you can write more efficient and optimized code.

1. Stack vs Heap

In Go, variables are either allocated on the **stack** or the **heap**. The stack is used for short-lived variables, while the heap is for variables that need to persist beyond the lifetime of a function call.

- **Stack Allocation:**

- Variables stored on the stack are automatically deallocated when the function in which they were defined returns. Stack allocation is fast because memory allocation and deallocation follow a Last-In-First-Out (LIFO) order.
- **Heap Allocation**:
- Variables that are used beyond the scope of the function in which they were created are allocated on the heap. The heap is managed by Go's garbage collector. Heap allocation is slower than stack allocation because the garbage collector must track and free memory that is no longer in use.

Example of stack and heap allocation:

```go
Copy code
package main

import "fmt"

type Person struct {
    name string
    age  int
}

func stackAllocated() int {
    x := 10 // Allocated on the stack
    return x
}

func heapAllocated() *Person {
    p := &Person{name: "Alice",
 age: 30} // Allocated on the heap
    return p
}

func main() {
    fmt.Println(stackAllocated())
```

```
    fmt.Println(heapAllocated())
}
```

In the example:

- x is allocated on the stack and destroyed when stackAllocated returns.
- The Person struct is allocated on the heap because it is returned as a pointer, and Go's runtime ensures it persists beyond the function call.

2. Escape Analysis

Go uses **escape analysis** to determine whether variables should be allocated on the stack or heap. If a variable is used outside the function that declares it, Go will "escape" it to the heap.

Escape analysis helps the Go runtime make efficient memory allocation decisions automatically, but understanding when a variable will escape to the heap can help you optimize your program.

Example:

```go
Copy code
func foo() *int {
    x := 42
    return &x // x escapes to the heap
}
```

In this example, x is allocated on the heap because it is returned as a pointer and accessed outside of foo.

Working with Pointers and Values

Go provides both **value types** and **pointer types**. Working with pointers is essential for efficient memory usage and for controlling how data is passed between functions.

1. Value Types vs Pointer Types

- **Value types**: When you pass a value type (e.g., int, struct) to a function, Go creates a copy of the value. Any modifications made inside the function do not affect the original value.

```go
Copy code
func modifyValue(x int) {
    x = 20
}

func main() {
    x := 10
    modifyValue(x)
    fmt.Println(x) // Still 10
}
```

- **Pointer types**: Pointers allow you to pass references to variables, meaning changes made to the variable inside a function will reflect outside the function.

```go
Copy code
func modifyPointer(x *int) {
    *x = 20
}

func main() {
    x := 10
    modifyPointer(&x)
    fmt.Println(x) // Now 20
}
```

Best practices:

- Use **value types** for small, short-lived data structures that do not need to be modified by multiple functions.

- Use **pointers** when you want to avoid copying large data structures or when the function needs to modify the original value.

2. Passing Pointers to Structs

Passing large structs by value can be inefficient, as it involves copying the entire struct. Using pointers allows you to pass a reference to the struct, avoiding unnecessary copies.

```go
Copy code
type LargeStruct struct {
    data [1000]int
}

func processLargeStruct(s *LargeStruct) {
    // Modifies the original struct
    s.data[0] = 42
}

func main() {
    ls := LargeStruct{}
    processLargeStruct(&ls)
// Pass by reference
}
```

Profiling and Benchmarking Go Code

Optimizing Go code often requires understanding where your program is spending time and how it is using memory. Go provides built-in tools like pprof and testing to help profile and benchmark your code.

1. Profiling with pprof

The pprof package allows you to profile your program's CPU and memory usage to identify bottlenecks.

How to use pprof:

1. Import net/http/pprof in your Go program:

71

```go
Copy code
import _ "net/http/pprof"
```

1. Start an HTTP server for profiling:

```go
Copy code
go func() {
    log.Println(http.ListenAndServe
("localhost:6060", nil))
}()
```

1. Run your program, then navigate to http://localhost:6060/debug/pprof/ to access CPU and memory profiles.
2. Use the go tool pprof command to analyze the profiles:

```bash
Copy code
go tool pprof http://localhost:6060/debug/pprof/profile
```

2. Benchmarking with the testing Package

Go's testing package includes functionality for writing benchmarks to measure performance.

Example of a benchmark function:

```go
Copy code
```

```
package main

import (
    "testing"
)

func BenchmarkExample(b *testing.B) {
    for i := 0; i < b.N; i++ {
        someFunction() //
 Code you want to benchmark
    }
}
```

Run the benchmark using:

```bash
Copy code
go test -bench=.
```

This will run the benchmark and provide performance data such as the number of operations per second and the average time per operation.

3. Heap and GC Profiling

You can profile memory allocations and garbage collection using the heap and gc profiles. This helps identify areas of your code where memory usage is high or where the garbage collector is doing extra work.

Heap profile:

```bash
Copy code
go tool pprof http:/
/localhost:6060/debug
/pprof/heap
```

GC trace (set GODEBUG environment variable):

```bash
Copy code
GODEBUG=gctrace=1 ./your-program
```

Avoiding Memory Leaks and Optimizing GC

Although Go's garbage collector takes care of most memory management issues, it's still important to avoid practices that can lead to memory leaks or excessive memory usage. Let's explore how to avoid common memory issues and optimize the performance of the garbage collector.

1. Avoiding Memory Leaks

Memory leaks occur when memory that is no longer needed is not released. This can happen when references to objects are inadvertently retained, preventing the garbage collector from freeing them.

Common causes of memory leaks in Go:

- **Unclosed resources**: Files, network connections, and database connections should always be closed after use.

```go
Copy code
f, err := os.Open("file.txt")
if err != nil {
    log.Fatal(err)
}
defer f.Close() // Always close resources
```

- **Dangling goroutines**: Goroutines that don't terminate can retain memory unnecessarily. Always ensure that goroutines are properly managed and have an exit condition.

```go
Copy code
func main() {
    done := make(chan bool)
    go func() {
        defer close(done)
        // Do some work
    }()
    <-done // Wait for goroutine to finish
}
```

- **Retaining slices**: If you need only part of a slice but hold on to the entire slice, you may retain more memory than necessary. Use the copy function to avoid retaining large backing arrays.

```go
Copy code
original := make([]byte, 10000)
smallSlice := original[:10]
// Still retains the entire array
// Avoid memory retention:
newSlice := make([]byte, 10)
copy(newSlice, smallSlice)
  // Only copy the required data
```

2. Optimizing Garbage Collection (GC)

Garbage collection is an important part of Go's memory management, but if not handled correctly, it can become a performance bottleneck.

Garbage Collection Basics:

- Go uses a **concurrent, mark-and-sweep garbage collector**. It identifies and frees memory that is no longer in use.
- The garbage collector runs periodically, but if your program allocates a lot of memory quickly, the garbage collector may run more often, which

75

can affect performance.

Tips for optimizing garbage collection:

- **Minimize allocations**: Avoid unnecessary allocations, especially inside loops. For example, reuse buffers and slices instead of creating new ones on each iteration.

```go
Copy code
buf := make([]byte, 1024)
for i := 0; i < 1000; i
```

Chapter 8: Testing in Go

T esting is a critical aspect of software development that ensures the correctness, reliability, and performance of your applications. Go offers a powerful built-in testing framework that simplifies the process of writing tests and integrating them into your development workflow. In this chapter, we will explore how to write unit tests using Go's testing package, the principles of Test-Driven Development (TDD), techniques for mocking and dependency injection, and methods for benchmarking and performance testing.

Writing Unit Tests with testing

Go's standard library includes the testing package, which provides the tools needed to write unit tests for your code. Unit tests are designed to verify that individual units of code (usually functions or methods) behave as expected.

1. Creating a Test File

To create a test file, follow these steps:

1. Create a file ending with _test.go in the same directory as the code you want to test. For example, if your code is in math.go, create math_test.go.
2. Import the testing package.

```go
go
Copy code
// math.go
package mathutil

func Add(a, b int) int {
    return a + b
}

// math_test.go
package mathutil

import "testing"

func TestAdd(t *testing.T) {
    result := Add(2, 3)
    expected := 5
    if result != expected {
        t.Errorf("Add(2, 3)
= %d; want %d", result, expected)
    }
}
```

2. Running Tests

To run your tests, use the go test command in the terminal:

```bash
bash
Copy code
go test
```

This command automatically discovers and runs all tests defined in files that end with _test.go.

3. Testing Functions

In addition to testing for expected values, you can also test for errors and edge cases. Here's an example of testing a function that might return an error:

```go
Copy code
func Divide(a, b float64) (float64, error) {
    if b == 0 {
        return 0, fmt.Errorf
("cannot divide by zero")
    }
    return a / b, nil
}

// Test for Divide function
func TestDivide(t *testing.T) {
    _, err := Divide(4, 0)
    if err == nil {
        t.Error
("Expected an error when dividing by zero")
    }
}
```

4. Table-Driven Tests

Table-driven tests are a common pattern in Go for testing multiple cases in a single test function. This approach keeps your tests organized and reduces code duplication.

```go
Copy code
func TestAddTableDriven(t *testing.T) {
    cases := []struct {
        a, b      int
        expected int
    }{
        {2, 3, 5},
        {1, 1, 2},
        {-1, 1, 0},
    }

    for _, c := range cases {
        result := Add(c.a, c.b)
```

```
    if result != c.expected {
        t.Errorf("Add(%d, %d)
= %d; want %d", c.a,
c.b, result, c.expected)
    }
  }
}
```

This pattern makes it easy to add new test cases by simply adding to the cases slice.

Test-Driven Development in Go

Test-Driven Development (TDD) is a software development approach in which tests are written before the code that implements the functionality. TDD promotes writing simple, testable code and helps ensure that new features are tested as they are developed.

1. The TDD Cycle

The TDD cycle generally follows these three steps:

1. **Red**: Write a test for a new feature or functionality that currently fails.
2. **Green**: Write the minimum amount of code necessary to make the test pass.
3. **Refactor**: Improve the code while ensuring that the test still passes.

Example of TDD Cycle:

Step 1: Red Start by writing a test for a function that doesn't exist yet.

```go
Copy code
func TestMultiply(t *testing.T) {
    result := Multiply(2, 3)
    expected := 6
    if result != expected {
        t.Errorf("Multiply(2, 3)
= %d; want %d", result, expected)
    }
```

```
}
```

Step 2: Green Now, write the simplest implementation to pass the test.

```go
Copy code
func Multiply(a, b int) int {
    return a * b
}
```

Step 3: Refactor If necessary, refactor the code while ensuring that all tests continue to pass.

TDD helps you think critically about your design before implementation, leading to cleaner, more maintainable code.

Mocking and Dependency Injection

When testing, especially in larger applications, it's important to isolate the unit being tested. Mocking and dependency injection allow you to replace real dependencies with controlled, simulated versions.

1. Mocking

Mocking involves creating a mock object that simulates the behavior of a real object. This is particularly useful when the real object is complex, slow, or has side effects (like network calls).

Example of Mocking: Let's say you have a service that fetches data from an external API. Instead of calling the real API in your tests, you can create a mock service.

```go
Copy code
type DataFetcher interface {
    FetchData() (string, error)
}

type MockDataFetcher struct{}

func (m *MockDataFetcher) FetchData()
```

```
(string, error) {
    return "mock data", nil
}

func UseFetcher(fetcher DataFetcher) string {
    data, _ := fetcher.FetchData()
    return data
}

// Test using the mock
func TestUseFetcher(t *testing.T) {
    mock := &MockDataFetcher{}
    result := UseFetcher(mock)
    expected := "mock data"
    if result != expected {
        t.Errorf("UseFetcher() =
%s; want %s", result, expected)
    }
}
```

2. Dependency Injection

Dependency injection is a design pattern that allows you to pass dependencies into a function or structure rather than hardcoding them. This approach makes testing easier by allowing you to provide mock dependencies.

Example of Dependency Injection:

```go
go
Copy code
type App struct {
    Fetcher DataFetcher
}

func (a *App) GetData() string {
    data, _ := a.Fetcher.FetchData()
    return data
}
```

```
// In the main function or when setting up the app:
app := &App{Fetcher: &MockDataFetcher{}}
```

By injecting dependencies, you can swap real implementations with mocks or stubs in your tests.

Benchmarking and Performance Testing

In addition to unit testing, Go provides tools for benchmarking code performance. Benchmarking allows you to measure the time complexity and efficiency of your functions, ensuring they meet performance requirements.

1. Writing Benchmark Tests

Benchmark tests in Go are defined similarly to unit tests but with a specific signature. Each benchmark function should start with Benchmark, and it should accept a pointer to testing.B.

Example of a Benchmark Test:

```go
go
Copy code
package mathutil

import (
    "testing"
)

func BenchmarkAdd(b *testing.B) {
    for i := 0; i < b.N; i++ {
        Add(2, 3)
    }
}
```

To run your benchmarks, use the following command:

```bash
bash
Copy code
go test -bench=.
```

This command runs all benchmarks in your test files and provides performance metrics.

2. Benchmarking Strategies

- **Use b.N**: The b.N variable represents the number of iterations for the benchmark. Go automatically determines how many iterations to run to get reliable measurements.
- **Avoid external dependencies**: Benchmark tests should ideally not depend on I/O operations or other slow processes, as they can skew the results.
- **Profile memory**: Use memory profiling along with benchmarking to understand memory usage patterns and identify areas for optimization.

3. Analyzing Benchmark Results

After running your benchmarks, Go provides a summary of the results, including the number of operations per second and the average time taken per operation. Analyzing this data helps you identify performance bottlenecks and areas for improvement.

Conclusion

Testing in Go is straightforward and powerful, enabling you to ensure the reliability and performance of your applications. By writing unit tests, embracing Test-Driven Development, using mocking and dependency injection, and incorporating benchmarking into your workflow, you can maintain a high standard of code quality. As your Go projects grow, leveraging these practices will be essential for managing complexity, ensuring performance, and maintaining the integrity of your code.

Chapter 9: Error Handling and Logging

Effective error handling and logging are critical components of building reliable and maintainable applications. Go takes a unique approach to error handling, emphasizing explicit checks and custom error types. Additionally, robust logging practices help developers trace issues and monitor application behavior. In this chapter, we will explore idiomatic error handling in Go, the use of custom error types and wrapping, and strategies for implementing logging in Go applications.

Idiomatic Error Handling with error

Go's error handling philosophy encourages developers to handle errors explicitly rather than using exceptions, which promotes clarity and maintainability in code.

1. Understanding the error Type

In Go, an error is a built-in interface that represents an error condition. The error interface is defined as follows:

```go
Copy code
type error interface {
    Error() string
}
```

Any type that implements the Error() method satisfies the error interface.

This simplicity allows developers to create and return custom error types while ensuring compatibility with the standard error handling pattern.

2. Returning Errors from Functions

Go functions that may encounter an error typically return a value along with an error type. The calling function is then responsible for checking the error and handling it appropriately.

Example:

```go
Copy code
package main

import (
    "fmt"
    "errors"
)

// Divide returns the result of dividing
a by b, or an error if b is zero.
func Divide(a, b float64) (float64, error) {
    if b == 0 {
        return 0, errors.New("division by zero")
    }
    return a / b, nil
}

func main() {
    result, err := Divide(4, 0)
    if err != nil {
        fmt.Println("Error:", err)
        return
    }
    fmt.Println("Result:", result)
}
```

In this example, the Divide function returns an error if the denominator is zero. The caller checks for the error before proceeding, ensuring that potential issues are handled gracefully.

3. Error Checking Best Practices

- **Check errors immediately**: It's best practice to check errors as soon as they are returned. This minimizes the chance of overlooking an error, especially in larger functions.

```go
Copy code
if err := doSomething(); err != nil {
    return fmt.Errorf
("doSomething failed: %w", err)
}
```

- **Use defer for cleanup**: When working with resources like files or network connections, use defer to ensure they are properly closed, even in the event of an error.

```go
Copy code
f, err := os.Open("file.txt")
if err != nil {
    return err
}
defer f.Close()
```

Custom Error Types and Wrapping Errors

Creating custom error types allows you to add context and additional information to errors, making debugging and error handling more informative. Go 1.13 introduced error wrapping, which allows you to create layered error messages while preserving the original error.

1. Defining Custom Error Types

Custom error types can include additional fields to convey more information about the error condition.

Example:

```go
Copy code
type MyError struct {
    Message string
    Code    int
}

func (e *MyError) Error() string {
    return fmt.Sprintf("Error %d: %s", e.Code, e.Message)
}

func doSomething() error {
    return &MyError{
        Message: "Something went wrong",
        Code:    500,
    }
}
```

Here, MyError includes both a message and a code, providing more context when the error occurs.

2. Error Wrapping

Go's error wrapping feature allows you to create new errors that include context while retaining the original error.

Example:

```go
Copy code
func main() {
    err := doSomething()
    if err != nil {
        wrappedErr := fmt.Errorf("failed to do something: %w", err)
        fmt.Println(wrappedErr) // The wrapped error includes the
        original error
    }
```

```
}
```

To unwrap the error later, you can use the errors.Unwrap function or errors.Is and errors.As to check for specific error types.

3. Checking for Specific Errors

Using the errors.Is and errors.As functions allows you to check for specific errors or extract custom error types from wrapped errors.

Example:

```go
go
Copy code
var myErr *MyError

if errors.As(err, &myErr) {
    fmt.Println("Caught a MyError:", myErr)
}
```

This approach allows you to write more flexible error handling logic that can differentiate between different error types, enabling fine-grained control over error responses.

Logging Strategies for Go Applications

Logging is an essential aspect of software development, providing insights into application behavior, performance, and potential issues. Effective logging practices help with debugging, monitoring, and maintaining the health of your applications.

1. The Importance of Logging

- **Debugging**: Logs can help trace issues and understand application behavior during development and production.
- **Monitoring**: Use logs to monitor the health and performance of applications in production environments.
- **Auditing**: Maintain logs for auditing purposes, ensuring compliance and tracking changes.

2. Using the log Package

Go's standard library includes the log package, which provides a simple logging interface.

Basic Usage:

```go
Copy code
import "log"

func main() {
    log.Println("This is a standard log message.")
    log.Fatal("This is a fatal log message, and the program will
    exit.") // Fatal logs and exits
}
```

Log Levels: While the standard log package does not provide built-in support for log levels (e.g., info, warning, error), you can create custom loggers or use third-party libraries like logrus or zap for more advanced logging features.

3. Structured Logging

Structured logging involves logging events with structured data (e.g., JSON), making it easier to search and analyze logs. This is particularly useful in distributed systems.

Example with logrus:

```go
Copy code
import (
    "github.com/sirupsen/logrus"
)

func main() {
    logger := logrus.New()
    logger.WithFields(logrus.Fields{
        "username": "john_doe",
        "action":   "login",
    }).Info("User logged in")
}
```

Structured logs can be easily parsed by log management tools and provide rich context for each log entry.

4. Log Rotation and Management

In production applications, consider implementing log rotation to manage log file sizes. Go's log package does not handle log rotation out of the box, so you may need to use third-party packages like lumberjack for this functionality.

Example with lumberjack:

```go
Copy code
import (
    "gopkg.in/natefinch/lumberjack.v2"
)

func main() {
    log.SetOutput(&lumberjack.Logger{
        Filename:   "app.log",
        MaxSize:    10, // megabytes
        MaxBackups: 5,
        MaxAge:     28, // days
    })
}
```

This example configures a logger that will manage log files, ensuring that old logs are deleted when the maximum size or age limit is reached.

5. Contextual Logging

When working with concurrent applications, contextual logging can help correlate log entries across different goroutines. You can use context to pass request-specific information (like request IDs) through your application.

Example with Context:

```go
Copy code
import (
    "context"
```

```
    "log"
)

func handler(ctx context.Context) {
    requestID := ctx.Value("requestID")
    log.Printf("Processing request %s", requestID)
}

func main() {
    ctx := context.WithValue
(context.Background(), "requestID", "12345")
    handler(ctx)
}
```

Using context allows you to maintain a clear trace of logs associated with specific requests, improving your ability to debug and monitor your application.

Conclusion

Effective error handling and logging are essential for developing robust and maintainable applications in Go. By adopting idiomatic error handling practices, such as using the error interface, creating custom error types, and employing error wrapping, you can ensure that errors are managed clearly and effectively. Coupling these practices with robust logging strategies—such as structured logging, log rotation, and contextual logging—will enhance your ability to monitor and troubleshoot your applications, leading to improved reliability and user experience.

Chapter 10: Security Best Practices in Go

S ecurity is a critical aspect of software development that must be considered at every stage of the application lifecycle. Go provides several features and libraries that can help developers write secure code and protect applications from common vulnerabilities. In this chapter, we will explore best practices for writing secure Go code, handling user input to prevent injection attacks, and managing secrets and sensitive data.

Writing Secure Go Code

Writing secure code starts with understanding common vulnerabilities and implementing best practices to mitigate them. Here are several key principles to follow when developing secure Go applications:

1. Validate Input Data

Always validate and sanitize user input. This helps prevent various attacks, such as SQL injection, command injection, and cross-site scripting (XSS). Go's strong type system can assist in enforcing data integrity, but additional checks are necessary for user input.

Example of Input Validation:

```go
go
Copy code
package main

import (
    "fmt"
    "net/http"
    "regexp"
)

func validateUsername(username string) error {
    // Regex to allow only alphanumeric characters
    if !regexp.MustCompile(`^[a-zA-Z0-9]+$`).MatchString(username)
    {
        return fmt.Errorf("invalid username: %s", username)
    }
    return nil
}

func handler(w http.ResponseWriter,
 r *http.Request) {
    username := r.URL.Query().
Get("username")
    if err := validateUsername
(username); err != nil {
        http.Error(w, err.Error(), http.StatusBadRequest)
        return
    }
    fmt.Fprintf(w, "Hello, %s!", username)
}
```

In this example, the username is validated against a regular expression to ensure it only contains alphanumeric characters.

2. Use HTTPS

Always use HTTPS to encrypt data in transit. This protects sensitive information, such as authentication tokens and user data, from being intercepted by attackers.

To enable HTTPS in a Go application, you can use the http.ListenAndServ eTLS function:

```go
Copy code
package main

import (
    "log"
    "net/http"
)

func main() {
    http.HandleFunc("/", handler)
    log.Fatal(http.ListenAndServeTLS(":443", "server.crt",
    "server.key", nil))
}
```

Ensure you have a valid SSL certificate, which you can obtain from a Certificate Authority (CA) or use a tool like Let's Encrypt for free certificates.

3. Limit Exposure of Sensitive Data

When handling sensitive data, ensure that it is not exposed unnecessarily. For example, avoid logging sensitive information and use environment variables to manage secrets.

Example of Managing Secrets:

```go
Copy code
import (
    "os"
)

func main() {
    dbPassword := os.Getenv("DB_PASSWORD")
    // Use dbPassword to connect to the database without exposing
    it in logs or source code
}
```

4. Error Handling

Avoid exposing detailed error messages that can leak sensitive information about your application's internals. Instead, return generic error messages to the user and log the details for debugging.

Example:

```go
Copy code
if err != nil {
    log.Println("Error connecting to
  database:", err) // Log detailed error
    http.Error(w, "Internal Server Error",
    http.StatusInternalServerError)
  // User-friendly error
}
```

Handling User Input and Preventing Injection Attacks

Injection attacks are among the most common vulnerabilities in web applications. These attacks occur when an attacker can send malicious input to the application, which is then executed by the database or shell.

1. SQL Injection Prevention

To prevent SQL injection, use parameterized queries or prepared statements instead of constructing SQL queries using string concatenation.

Example with database/sql:

```go
Copy code
import (
    "database/sql"
    _ "github.com/go-sql-driver/mysql"
)

func getUserByID(db *sql.DB, id int)
  (*User, error) {
    var user User
    err := db.QueryRow("SELECT id,
  username FROM users WHERE id = ?",
  id).Scan(&user.ID, &user.Username)
```

```
if err != nil {
    return nil, err
}
return &user, nil
}
```

In this example, the ? placeholder is used to safely bind the id parameter, preventing SQL injection.

2. Cross-Site Scripting (XSS) Prevention

To prevent XSS attacks, always escape user-generated content before rendering it in HTML. Use Go's built-in html package to sanitize output.

Example:

```go
Copy code
import (
    "html/template"
    "net/http"
)

func handler(w http.ResponseWriter,
r *http.Request) {
    username := r.URL.Query().
Get("username")
    tmpl := template.Must(template.New
("greet").Parse("<h1>Hello, {{.}}</h1>"))
    tmpl.Execute(w, template.HTMLEscapeString(username))
  // Escape user input
}
```

This code uses template.HTMLEscapeString to ensure that any special HTML characters in username are escaped.

3. Command Injection Prevention

When executing shell commands, always validate and sanitize inputs, or use Go libraries that do not require shell invocation. Avoid using os/exec with user input.

Example of safe command execution:

```go
Copy code
import (
    "os/exec"
)

func runCommand(command string,
  args []string) error {
    cmd := exec.Command(command,
  args...) // Use a safe command without user input
    return cmd.Run()
}
```

By avoiding the direct inclusion of user input in command execution, you mitigate the risk of command injection.

Managing Secrets and Sensitive Data

Handling secrets, such as API keys, passwords, and database credentials, securely is vital for protecting your applications. Go offers various strategies and best practices for managing sensitive data.

1. Environment Variables

Storing sensitive information in environment variables is a common practice. This keeps secrets out of your codebase and allows for easier configuration across different environments (development, staging, production).

Example of Reading Environment Variables:

```go
Copy code
package main

import (
    "os"
)

func main() {
```

```
    apiKey := os.Getenv("API_KEY")
    // Use apiKey securely
  without exposing it in source code
}
```

To set environment variables, you can use the terminal:

```bash
bash
Copy code
export API_KEY="your_secret_api_key"
```

2. Using Configuration Files

If you prefer using configuration files, ensure they are not included in version control. Use .gitignore to exclude files containing sensitive data. Consider using libraries that support encryption for configuration files.

Example with viper:

```go
go
Copy code
import (
    "github.com/spf13/viper"
)

func main() {
    viper.SetConfigName("config")
  // name of config file (without extension)
    viper.SetConfigType("yaml")
  // required if the config file is not .json
    viper.AddConfigPath(".")
   // optionally look for config in the working directory

    if err := viper.ReadInConfig();
  err != nil {
        panic(err) // Handle the error
    }
```

```go
    apiKey := viper.GetString("API_KEY")
  // Retrieve the API key from the config file
}
```

3. Secret Management Services

For production environments, consider using secret management services such as HashiCorp Vault, AWS Secrets Manager, or Azure Key Vault. These services provide a secure way to store and access secrets without hardcoding them in your application.

Example with HashiCorp Vault:

Using the Vault client library for Go, you can access secrets securely:

```go
go
Copy code
import (
    "github.com/hashicorp/vault/api"
)

func main() {
    client, err := api.NewClient
(api.DefaultConfig())
    if err != nil {
        // Handle error
    }

    secret, err := client.Logical().Read("secret/my_secret")
    if err != nil {
        // Handle error
    }
    apiKey := secret.Data
["API_KEY"].(string)
// Retrieve the API key securely
}
```

Using a secret management service not only secures your sensitive data but also centralizes management and auditing of secrets.

Conclusion

Security is a fundamental aspect of software development that must be prioritized from the outset. By adopting idiomatic error handling practices, ensuring safe handling of user input, and implementing effective strategies for managing secrets, you can significantly reduce the risk of vulnerabilities in your Go applications. The principles outlined in this chapter will help you build more secure applications, protect sensitive data, and maintain user trust.

Chapter 11: Deploying and Scaling Go Applications

Deploying and scaling applications effectively is crucial for ensuring performance, reliability, and maintainability in production environments. Go's design features make it well-suited for building scalable applications, but deploying them requires careful planning and adherence to best practices. This chapter covers best practices for building production-ready Go applications, handling configuration, implementing monitoring and observability, and deploying to cloud and containerized environments.

Building for Production: Best Practices

When preparing a Go application for production, several best practices can help ensure that the application runs efficiently and reliably.

1. Build Optimization

- **Compile with optimizations**: Use the -ldflags flag to reduce binary size and optimize performance during the build process.

```bash
Copy code
```

```
go build -ldflags="-s -w" -o myapp
```

- The -s and -w flags omit the symbol table and debug information, reducing the size of the final binary.
- **Use Go Modules**: Ensure that you're using Go Modules to manage dependencies, as this promotes reproducibility and reduces issues with dependency conflicts.

2. Static Linking

Go binaries are statically linked by default, meaning that all dependencies are included in the compiled binary. This simplifies deployment since there are no external dependencies to manage.

- **Build a static binary**:

```bash
Copy code
CGO_ENABLED=0 GOOS=linux GOARCH=amd64
go build -o myapp
```

Setting CGO_ENABLED=0 ensures that no C dependencies are linked, resulting in a fully static binary.

3. Security Considerations

- **Use go mod tidy**: Before deployment, run go mod tidy to ensure your go.mod file is clean and only includes necessary dependencies.
- **Regularly update dependencies**: Keep dependencies up to date to benefit from security patches and performance improvements. Use tools like go get -u to update dependencies.
- **Scan for vulnerabilities**: Use tools like gosec or staticcheck to analyze your code for potential security issues.

4. Graceful Shutdown

Implement graceful shutdowns in your application to handle ongoing requests before shutting down. This is particularly important in web services and APIs.

Example of graceful shutdown:

```go
Copy code
package main

import (
    "context"
    "log"
    "net/http"
    "os"
    "os/signal"
    "syscall"
    "time"
)

func main() {
    srv := &http.Server{Addr: ":8080"}

    // Handle signals for graceful shutdown
    go func() {
        c := make(chan os.Signal, 1)
        signal.Notify(c, syscall.SIGINT,
syscall.SIGTERM)
        <-c // Wait for a signal
        ctx, cancel := context.
WithTimeout(context.
Background(), 5*time.Second)
        defer cancel()
        srv.Shutdown(ctx)
// Shutdown the server gracefully
    }()

    log.Println("Starting server on :8080")
    if err := srv.ListenAndServe();
```

```
err != nil && err != http.ErrServerClosed {
        log.Fatalf("ListenAndServe: %v", err)
    }
}
```

This code listens for termination signals and shuts down the server gracefully, allowing it to complete any ongoing requests.

Handling Environment Variables and Configuration

Configuration management is crucial for ensuring that your application runs correctly in different environments (development, testing, production). Using environment variables is a common and effective approach.

1. Using Environment Variables

Environment variables provide a flexible way to manage configuration without hardcoding values in your source code. You can use the os package to read environment variables.

Example:

```go
go
Copy code
package main

import (
    "fmt"
    "os"
)

func main() {
    dbPassword := os.Getenv("DB_PASSWORD")
    if dbPassword == "" {
        fmt.Println("DB_PASSWORD is not set")
        return
    }
    // Use dbPassword to connect to the database
}
```

2. Configuration Management Libraries

Consider using configuration management libraries like viper or go-configuration to manage configuration settings more effectively. These libraries support reading from various sources, including JSON, YAML, and environment variables.

Example with viper:

```go
Copy code
import (
    "github.com/spf13/viper"
)

func main() {
    viper.SetConfigName("config")
// Name of the config file
    viper.SetConfigType("yaml")
 // File type
    viper.AddConfigPath(".")
   // Path to look for the config file

    if err := viper.ReadInConfig
(); err != nil {
        panic(err)
    }

    dbPassword := viper.
GetString("DB_PASSWORD")
    // Use dbPassword as needed
}
```

This allows for a more organized and maintainable way to manage configuration.

Monitoring and Observability with Go Applications

Monitoring and observability are essential for maintaining the health and performance of your applications in production. Implementing logging, metrics, and tracing will help you gain insights into your application's behavior and performance.

1. Logging

Use structured logging to capture key information about application behavior and errors. Structured logs provide context and can be easily parsed by log management systems.

Example with logrus:

```go
Copy code
import (
    "github.com/sirupsen/logrus"
)

func main() {
    logger := logrus.New()
    logger.WithFields(logrus.Fields{
        "username": "johndoe",
        "action":   "login",
    }).Info("User logged in")
}
```

Structured logging allows you to search and analyze logs more effectively.

2. Metrics

Integrate a metrics collection library like Prometheus to gather performance metrics. This can include response times, request counts, error rates, and resource utilization.

Example with prometheus library:

```go
Copy code
import (
    "github.com/prometheus/client_
golang/prometheus"
    "github.com/prometheus/client_
golang/prometheus/promhttp"
    "net/http"
)

var (
```

```
    requestCount = prometheus.NewCounterVec(
        prometheus.CounterOpts{
            Name: "http_requests_total",
            Help: "Total number of
HTTP requests",
        },
        []string{"method"},
    )
)

func init() {
    prometheus.MustRegister(requestCount)
}

func handler(w http.ResponseWriter,
 r *http.Request) {
    requestCount.WithLabelValues
(r.Method).Inc()
    // Handle the request
}

func main() {
    http.Handle("/metrics",
 promhttp.Handler())
    http.HandleFunc("/", handler)
    http.ListenAndServe(":8080", nil)
}
```

In this example, a counter metric is created to track the total number of HTTP requests, which can be exposed at the /metrics endpoint for Prometheus to scrape.

3. Distributed Tracing

In microservices architectures, distributed tracing helps track requests as they propagate through multiple services. Libraries like OpenTelemetry or Jaeger can be used to instrument your Go applications for tracing.

Example with OpenTelemetry:

```go
go
Copy code
import (
    "go.opentelemetry.io/contrib/
instrumentation/net/http"
    "go.opentelemetry.io/otel"
)

func main() {
    // Setup OpenTelemetry
    tracer := otel.Tracer
("example.com/trace")

    httpTransport := httptrace.NewTransport
(http.DefaultTransport)

    client := &http.Client{Transport: httpTransport}
    // Use client for making requests with tracing
}
```

Using OpenTelemetry, you can gain visibility into the flow of requests across distributed systems, making it easier to diagnose performance bottlenecks and errors.

Deploying to Cloud and Containerized Environments

Cloud and containerized environments offer flexibility, scalability, and ease of deployment for Go applications. Understanding how to effectively deploy your Go applications in these environments is crucial for operational success.

1. Deploying to Cloud Platforms

Cloud providers like AWS, Google Cloud, and Azure offer various services for deploying Go applications. You can choose between several options:

- **Container orchestration**: Use services like Kubernetes to deploy and manage your Go applications in containers. This provides features like scaling, load balancing, and self-healing.
- **Serverless platforms**: Consider using serverless frameworks like AWS

Lambda or Google Cloud Functions to run Go applications without managing servers. This is ideal for event-driven applications.

Example of deploying with AWS Lambda:

1. Write your Go application and compile it for AWS Lambda:

```bash
Copy code
GOOS=linux GOARCH=amd64 go build -o main main.go
```

1. Create a deployment package:

```bash
Copy code
zip deployment.zip main
```

1. Deploy the function using AWS CLI:

```bash
Copy code
aws lambda create-function --function-name my-go-function
--zip-file fileb://deployment.zip --handler main --runtime go1.x
--role arn:aws:iam::ACCOUNT_ID:role/lambda-execution-role
```

2. Deploying with Docker

Docker is an excellent tool for containerizing Go applications, allowing you to run them consistently across various environments.

Creating a Dockerfile:

```
Dockerfile
Copy code
# Start from the official Go image
FROM golang:1.18 as builder

# Set the working directory
WORKDIR /app

# Copy the Go modules and install dependencies
COPY go.mod go.sum ./
RUN go mod download

# Copy the source code
COPY . .

# Build the Go application
RUN CGO_ENABLED=0 GOOS=linux GOARCH=amd64 go build -o myapp

# Create a minimal image for production
FROM alpine:latest
WORKDIR /root/
COPY --from=builder /app/myapp .

# Command to run the executable
CMD ["./myapp"]
```

Build and run the Docker container:

```bash
bash
Copy code
docker build -t my-go-app .
docker run -p 8080:8080 my-go-app
```

Using Docker ensures that your application runs in the same environment regardless of where it is deployed.

3. Continuous Integration/Continuous Deployment (CI/CD)

Implementing CI/CD pipelines can automate the deployment of your Go applications, ensuring that new features and fixes are deployed quickly and reliably.

Common CI/CD tools:

- **GitHub Actions**: Automate your build and deployment workflow directly from your GitHub repository.
- **GitLab CI/CD**: Built-in CI/CD capabilities in GitLab for automating the deployment process.
- **Jenkins**: A popular open-source automation server for building, testing, and deploying applications.

Example GitHub Action for Go:

```yaml
Copy code
name: Go CI

on:
  push:
    branches: [ main ]
  pull_request:
    branches: [ main ]

jobs:
  build:
    runs-on: ubuntu-latest

    steps:
    - name: Checkout code
      uses: actions/checkout@v2

    - name: Set up Go
      uses: actions/setup-go@v2
      with:
        go-version: '1.18'

    - name: Install dependencies
      run: go mod tidy
```

```
- name: Run tests
  run: go test ./...
```

This action automatically runs tests on every push or pull request, ensuring code quality and reliability before deployment.

Conclusion

Deploying and scaling Go applications effectively requires a solid understanding of best practices for building production-ready code, managing configuration, and implementing monitoring and observability. By leveraging cloud and containerized environments, you can take advantage of modern deployment strategies that enhance your application's reliability and scalability. Incorporating these practices into your development workflow will help ensure the success of your Go applications in production.

Chapter 12: The Future of Go

The Go programming language has continued to evolve since its inception, with ongoing developments and community contributions driving its growth. Understanding the future of Go, including upcoming features, how to keep your skills up to date, and the resources available within the Go community, is essential for any developer looking to stay relevant in the ever-changing landscape of software development. In this chapter, we will explore the anticipated changes in Go 2.0, ways to keep your Go skills sharp, and resources within the Go community for learning and collaboration.

Go 2.0 and What's Coming Next

The Go team has been discussing the potential for Go 2.0, focusing on improvements and new features that will enhance the language's usability and performance. While Go 2.0 is still in the conceptual stage, there are several proposed changes and enhancements that are being considered.

1. Potential Language Improvements

- **Generics**: One of the most significant features that have been widely discussed for Go 2.0 is the introduction of generics. Generics would allow developers to write functions and data structures that can operate on different types without sacrificing type safety. This feature aims to improve code reusability and reduce code duplication.
- **Example of Generics in Go**:

```go
go
Copy code
func Print[T any](value T) {
    fmt.Println(value)
}
```

- **Error Handling Enhancements**: Improving the error handling mechanism has been a topic of discussion. While the current error handling approach using return values is explicit, it can lead to verbose code. Future iterations might explore more elegant patterns for error handling.
- **Package Management Improvements**: Ongoing discussions about enhancing module management, including versioning and dependency management, aim to streamline the developer experience and reduce friction when working with dependencies.

2. Performance Enhancements

- **Garbage Collection Improvements**: As applications grow and become more complex, garbage collection becomes crucial for maintaining performance. Future versions of Go may introduce optimizations to the garbage collector to improve memory management efficiency and reduce latency.
- **Concurrency Model Enhancements**: The Go team continuously explores ways to enhance the concurrency model, ensuring that it remains effective for modern multicore processors and large-scale applications.

3. Backward Compatibility

One of Go's primary goals has been to maintain backward compatibility, allowing developers to upgrade to new versions without needing to rewrite their existing code. Any changes proposed for Go 2.0 will be approached with careful consideration of their impact on existing codebases.

Keeping Your Go Skills Up to Date

In the rapidly evolving world of software development, it's vital to keep your skills sharp and stay informed about the latest trends, features, and best practices in Go.

1. Official Go Documentation and Blogs

The official Go website (golang.org) is a treasure trove of information, offering comprehensive documentation, tutorials, and guides. Additionally, the Go Blog provides updates on new features, best practices, and insights from the Go community.

2. Online Courses and Tutorials

Many platforms offer online courses focused on Go programming, catering to various skill levels—from beginners to advanced developers. Websites like Coursera, Udemy, and Pluralsight frequently update their courses to reflect the latest changes in the language.

3. Books and Publications

Several books on Go cover different aspects of the language and its ecosystem. Look for newly published titles to learn about the latest developments and best practices.

Recommended Books:

- *The Go Programming Language* by Alan A. A. Donovan and Brian W. Kernighan
- *Go in Action* by William Kennedy, Brian Ketelsen, and Erik St. Martin
- *Concurrency in Go* by Katherine Cox-Buday

4. Community Engagement

Participating in the Go community can help you learn from others, share your knowledge, and stay updated on new trends. Consider joining:

- **Online forums and discussion groups**: Engage with other Go developers on platforms like Reddit, Stack Overflow, and the Golang Slack community.
- **Meetups and conferences**: Attend Go-related events, both local and

global, to network with fellow developers and gain insights from industry experts. Events like GopherCon provide a platform for learning and sharing knowledge.

The Go Community: Resources, Tools, and Contributions

The Go community is vibrant and active, with many resources and tools available to help developers collaborate, learn, and contribute to the language's growth.

1. Go Community Resources

- **Go Forum**: An online forum where Go developers can ask questions, share knowledge, and discuss topics related to the language.
- **Gopher Slack**: A Slack community for Go developers to connect, share, and collaborate on projects and ideas.

2. Tools and Libraries

- **Go Tools**: The Go ecosystem includes numerous tools for development, testing, and deployment, such as:
- **GoLand**: A powerful IDE from JetBrains tailored for Go development.
- **Visual Studio Code**: A lightweight code editor with Go extensions for enhanced productivity.
- **Delve**: A debugger for Go, allowing you to inspect variables, set breakpoints, and step through code.
- **Popular Libraries**: Familiarize yourself with popular Go libraries that can help you build robust applications more efficiently. Some notable libraries include:
- **Gin**: A lightweight web framework for building APIs.
- **Gorm**: An ORM (Object-Relational Mapping) library for working with databases.
- **Cobra**: A library for creating command-line applications.

3. Contributing to Go

Contributing to the Go project or its libraries is a great way to enhance your skills and give back to the community. You can contribute in various ways:

- **Report issues**: Help improve Go by reporting bugs and issues you encounter.
- **Submit pull requests**: If you identify areas for improvement or bugs in existing libraries, contribute fixes through pull requests.
- **Documentation**: Contributing to documentation is a valuable way to help others and improve your understanding of the language.

How to Contribute:

- Follow the Go contribution guidelines available on the official Go GitHub repository.
- Engage with maintainers and other contributors through GitHub discussions and issues.

Conclusion

The future of Go holds exciting possibilities with ongoing developments aimed at enhancing the language and its ecosystem. By staying informed about upcoming features, continuously improving your skills, and engaging with the Go community, you can position yourself as a proficient Go developer ready to tackle the challenges of modern software development. Embracing the resources and tools available within the Go community will empower you to contribute meaningfully and stay ahead in your programming journey.

Conclusion

Go has established itself as a powerful and efficient programming language that excels in building scalable, high-performance applications. Throughout this book, we have explored the core concepts of Go, from its syntax and concurrency model to advanced topics such as error handling, logging, testing, and deployment strategies.

As you continue your journey with Go, remember the following key takeaways:

1. **Embrace Idiomatic Practices**: Adhering to Go's conventions and best practices enhances code readability and maintainability. This includes effective error handling, structured logging, and the use of Go's powerful concurrency model.

2. **Prioritize Testing**: Testing is integral to ensuring the reliability of your applications. Utilize Go's testing tools, engage in Test-Driven Development (TDD), and implement robust benchmarking and profiling to maintain high code quality.

3. **Stay Informed and Engaged**: The Go community is vibrant and continuously evolving. Keeping your skills up to date through documentation, online resources, and community involvement will help you remain relevant in the ever-changing landscape of software development.

4. **Focus on Security**: Security should be a priority from the outset. Implement best practices for error handling, input validation, and

the management of sensitive data to protect your applications from vulnerabilities.

5. **Leverage Modern Deployment Practices**: As applications grow and scale, understanding deployment strategies for cloud and containerized environments is essential. Use tools like Docker, Kubernetes, and CI/CD pipelines to streamline deployment and ensure reliability.

The future of Go promises further enhancements and features that will continue to improve developer experience and application performance. By embracing these principles and actively participating in the Go community, you can contribute to the language's growth while building robust applications that meet the demands of users today and in the future.

Thank you for embarking on this journey to learn about Go. With a solid foundation and a commitment to continuous learning, you are well-equipped to tackle your next project with confidence and creativity. Happy coding!

www.ingramcontent.com/pod-product-compliance
Lightning Source LLC
Chambersburg PA
CBHW071517220526
45472CB00003B/1054